Principles
in Practice

The Principles in Practice imprint offers teachers concrete illustrations of effective classroom practices based in NCTE research briefs and policy statements. Each book discusses the research on a specific topic, links the research to an NCTE brief or policy statement, and then demonstrates how those principles come alive in practice: by showcasing actual classroom practices that demonstrate the policies in action; by talking about research in practical, teacher-friendly language; and by offering teachers possibilities for rethinking their own practices in light of the ideas presented in the books. Books within the imprint are grouped in strands, each strand focused on a significant topic of interest.

Volumes in the Adolescent Literacy Strand

Adolescent Literacy at Risk? The Impact of Standards (2009) Rebecca Bowers Sipe

Adolescents and Digital Literacies: Learning Alongside Our Students (2010) Sara Kajder

Adolescent Literacy and the Teaching of Reading: Lessons for Teachers of Literature (2010) Deborah Appleman

Volumes in the Writing in Today's Classrooms Strand

Writing in the Dialogical Classroom: Students and Teachers Responding to the Texts of Their Lives (2011) Bob Fecho

Becoming Writers in the Elementary Classroom: Visions and Decisions (2011) Katie Van Sluys

Writing Instruction in the Culturally Relevant Classroom (2011) Maisha T. Winn and Latrise P. Johnson

Volumes in the Literacy Assessment Strand

Our Better Judgment: Teacher Leadership for Writing Assessment (2012) Chris W. Gallagher and Eric D. Turley

D1504891

Our Better Judgment

Teacher Leadership for Writing Assessment

Chris W. Gallagher
Northeastern University

Eric D. Turley
Kirkwood High School
Kirkwood, Missouri

National Council of Teachers of English
1111 W. Kenyon Road, Urbana, Illinois 61801-1096

Staff Editors: Bonny Graham

Imprint Editor: Cathy Fleischer

Interior Design: Victoria Pohlmann

Cover Design: Pat Mayer

Cover and Chapter Photos: Robyn Stellhorn

NCTE Stock Number: 34764

Library of Congress Cataloging-in-Publication Data

Gallagher, Chris W.
  Our better judgment : teacher leadership for writing assessment / Chris W. Gallagher, Northeastern University, Eric D. Turley, Kirkwood High School, Kirkwood, Missouri.
       pages cm
  Includes bibliographical references and index.
  ISBN 978-0-8141-3476-4 (pbk)
  1. English language—Writing—Study and teaching (Secondary) 2. English language—Written English—Study and teaching (Secondary). I. Turley, Eric D. II. Title.
  LB1631.G1575 2012
  808'.0420712—dc23
                                                                    2012016189

Contents

Acknowledgments

Above all, we thank the teachers and students whose work is included in these pages. We are grateful to have been invited into their teaching and learning, and we are honored to share their wisdom with our readers. We also thank Cathy Fleischer for her encouragement to write this book in the first place and for her support and good counsel throughout the process. We also received excellent advice from NCTE's anonymous readers, to whom we extend our thanks.

In addition, Chris thanks his family—Molly, Cady, and Erin—for putting up with him. Special thanks this time to Erin, an inspiring and inspired writer. Chris is also grateful to Peter Elbow, Maja Wilson, Carmen Kynard, Kerri Franklin, Michelle Hite, and all the participants of the summer 2011 writing symposium in Amherst, Massachusetts, for their feedback and support. Finally, he is indebted to his friends working on the Quality Performance Assessment Initiative at the Center for Collaborative Education in Boston for putting him in touch with such wonderful teachers.

Eric thanks his colleagues at Kirkwood High School and Eureka High School for their enthusiastic encouragement of this project. Most of all, he thanks his family—Julie, Alex, and Katelyn—for their love and support.

Standards for the Assessment of Reading and Writing, Revised Edition

A publication of the IRA–NCTE Joint Task Force on Assessment

Introduction

This document provides a set of standards to guide decisions about assessing the teaching and learning of literacy. In the past 30 years, research has produced revolutionary changes in our understanding of language, learning, and the complex literacy demands of our rapidly changing society. The standards proposed in this document are intended to reflect these advances in our understanding.

Readers of this document most likely share common experiences with respect to literacy and assessment. For example, in our own school days, we were directed to read to get the correct meaning of a text so that we could answer questions put to us by someone who already knew that correct meaning or by a test (often multiple choice) for which the correct answers were already determined. In order to develop assessment practices that serve students in an increasingly complex society, we must outgrow the limitations of our own schooling histories and understand language, literacy, and assessment in more complex ways. Literacy involves not just reading and writing, but a wide range of related language activities. It is both more social and more personal than a mere set of skills.

The need to understand language is particularly important. Language is not only the object of assessment but also part of the process of assessment. Consequently, any discussion of literacy assessment must include a discussion of language—what it is, how it is learned, and how it relates to assessment. Before we state our assessment standards, then, we will give an overview of what we mean by assessment and how we understand language and its relationship to assessment.

The Nature of Assessment

For many years, a transmission view of knowledge, curriculum, and assessment dominated and appeared to satisfy our social, political, and economic needs. Knowledge was regarded as a static entity that was "out there" somewhere, so the key educational question was, How do you get it from out there into students' heads? The corollary assessment question was, What counts as evidence that the knowledge really is in their heads? In a transmission view, it made sense to develop educational standards that specified the content of instruction before developing assessment procedures and engagements.

In the 1920s, notions of the basic purposes of schooling began to shift from an emphasis on the transmission of knowledge to the more complex nurturing of independent and collaborative learning and of problem solving. This shift has gained increasing prominence in today's postindustrial society, with its ever-expanding need for workers with strong communication skills and dispositions toward problem solving and collaborating. A curriculum committed to independent learning is built on the premise that inquiry, rather than mere transmission of knowledge, is the basis of teaching and learning.

Standards for the Assessment of Reading and Writing

This shift from knowledge transmission to inquiry as a primary goal of schools has important implications for assessment. In a knowledge-transmission framework, tests of static knowledge can suffice as assessment instruments. Students are the participants who are primarily accountable (either they have the knowledge or they don't), with teachers held accountable next. Policymakers, including school board members, trustees, or regents, are the primary recipients of assessment data. An inquiry framework changes the role of assessment and the roles of the participants. Within this framework, assessment is the exploration of how the educational environment and the participants in the educational community support the process of students as they learn to become independent and collaborative thinkers and problem solvers. This exploration includes an examination of the environment for teaching and learning, the processes and products of learning, and the degree to which all participants—students, teachers, administrators, parents, and board members—meet their obligation to support inquiry. Such assessments examine not only learning over time but also the contexts of learning.

Inquiry emphasizes different processes and types of knowledge than does knowledge transmission. For example, it values the ability to recognize problems and to generate multiple and diverse perspectives in trying to solve them. An inquiry stance asserts that while knowledge and language are likely to change over time, the need for learners at all levels (students, teachers, parents, administrators, and policymakers) who can solve new problems, generate new knowledge, and invent new language practices will remain constant. An inquiry perspective promotes problem posing and problem solving as goals for all participants in the educational community. For example, inquiry values the question of how information from different sources can be used to solve a particular problem. It values explorations of how teachers can promote critical thinking for all students. And it raises the question of why our society privileges the knowledge and cultural heritage of some groups over others within current school settings.

Inquiry fits the needs of a multicultural society in which it is essential to value and find strength in cultural diversity. It also honors the commitment to raising questions and generating multiple solutions. Various stakeholders and cultural groups provide different answers and new perspectives on problems. Respecting difference among learners enriches the curriculum and reduces the likelihood of problematic curricular narrowing.

Just as the principle of inquiry values difference, so the principle of difference values conversation over recitation as the primary mode of discourse. In a recitation, it is assumed that one person, the teacher, possesses the answers and that the others, the students, interact with the teacher and one another in an attempt to uncover the teacher's knowledge. In a conversation, all of the stakeholders in the educational environment (students, parents, teachers, specialists, administrators, and policymakers) have a voice at the table as curriculum, standards, and assessments are negotiated. Neither inquiry nor learning is viewed as the exclusive domain of students and teachers; both are primary concerns for all members of the school community. For example, administrators ask themselves hard questions about whether the structures they have established support staff development, teacher reflection, and student learning. School board members ask themselves whether they have lived up to the standards they have set for themselves and their schools to provide teachers and students with the resources they need to guarantee learning opportunities.

Quality assessment, then, hinges on the process of setting up conditions so that the classroom, the school, and the community become centers of inquiry where students, teachers, and other members of the school community investigate their own learning, both individually and collaboratively. The onus of assessment does not fall disproportionately upon students and teachers (which is often the case in schools today); instead, all those inquiring into the nature and effectiveness of educational practices are responsible for investigating the roles they have played. Different members of the school community have different but interacting interests, roles, and responsibilities, and assessment is the medium that allows all to explore what they have learned and whether they have met their responsibilities to the school community.

The Nature of Language

Language is very much like a living organism. It cannot be put together from parts like a machine, and it is constantly changing. Like a living organism, it exists only in interaction with others, in a social interdependence. Language is a system of signs through and within which we represent and make sense of the world and of ourselves. Language does not contain meaning; rather, meaning is constructed in the social relationships within which language is used. Individuals make sense of language within their social relationships, their personal histories, and their collective memory. In order to make sense of even a single word, people take into account the situation and their relationship with the speaker or writer.

Take, for example, *family*, a word often used as if all members of society agree on its meaning. The word may mean different things in different contexts, however, whether cultural, situational, or personal. To a middle-aged white person whose parents moved across country with their two children and who repeated that experience herself, *family* may mean the nuclear family structure in which she grew up and in which she is raising her own children. To someone from a different culture—perhaps an African American or Asian American—the word may conjure images of the constellation of grandparents, aunts, uncles, and cousins who live together or near one another. So, meaning may vary from one person to another, as in this case, where meanings attached to the word *family* are likely to differ depending on one's own experience in the family or families one has lived with. Thus, individuals make different sense of apparently similar language to the extent that their cultural and personal histories do not coincide. Consequently, when we attempt to standardize a test (by making it the same for everyone), we make the tenuous assumption that students will all make the same meaning from the language of our instructions and the language of the individual items.

Different cultures also have different ways of representing the world, themselves, and their intentions with language. For example, in any given cultural group, people have different ways of greeting one another, depending on the situation (e.g., a business meeting, a funeral, a date) and on their relationship to each other. Our own language practices come from our cultural experience, but they are also part of the collective practice that forms the culture. Indeed, the different ways people use language to make sense of the world and of their lives are the major distinguishing features of different cultural groups.

At the same time, language is always changing as we use it. Words acquire different meanings, and new language structures and uses appear as people stretch and pull the language to make new meanings. Consequently, the meaning that individuals make from language varies across time, social situation, personal perspective, and cultural group.

The Nature of Literacy

The nature of literacy is also continually changing. Today, many children read more online than offline. They are growing into a digital world in which relatively little reading and writing involves paper, most reading and writing involves images as much as print, and writing (both formal and less formal, the latter including e-mail, texts, Facebook posts, etc.) is becoming equal to, or even supplanting, reading as a primary literacy engagement. The tools of literacy are changing rapidly as new forms of Internet communication technology (ICT) are created, including (at the time of writing) bulletin boards, Web editors, blogs, virtual worlds, and social networking sites such as Ning and MySpace. The social practices of literacy also change as a result of using digital technologies, as does the development of language. New literate practices are learned and refined just by existing from day to day in what has become known as the mediasphere. For example, living with cell phones leads to texting, which changes how people view writing and how they write, and frequenting Web 2.0 sites, such as the video-sharing service YouTube, privileges a visual mode and shapes both attention to and facility with other modes of meaning making. The literacies children encounter by the end of their schooling were unimagined when they began.

Reading and writing online changes what it means to read, write, and comprehend. Literacy practices now involve both the creation and use of multimodal texts (broadly defined). Creating multimodal texts requires knowing the properties and limitations of different digital tools so that decisions can be made about how best to serve one's intentions. Participating in social networking sites, for example, requires new literacy practices; new literacy practices shape how users are perceived and how they construct identities. This leads to new areas needing to be assessed, including how youths create and enhance multiple identities using digital tools and virtual spaces. We now need to be concerned with teaching and assessing how students take an idea in print and represent it with video clips for other audiences. Similarly, we must be concerned about the stances and practices involved in taking an idea presented in one modality (e.g., print) and transcribing or transmediating it into another (e.g., digital video), and we must consider what possibilities and limitations a particular mode offers and how that relates to its desirability over other modes for particular purposes and situations. Children use different comprehension strategies online and offline, and assessments of the two show different pictures of their literacy development. Online readers, by choosing hypertext and intertext links, actually construct the texts that they read as well as the meanings they make. New multimodal texts require new critical media literacies, linked to classical critical literacy notions of how media culture is created, appropriated, and subsequently colonizes the broader notions of culture—for example, how youth culture is defined by and used to define what youths do, what they buy, and with whom they associate.

Standards for the Assessment of Reading and Writing

The definitions of literacy that have dominated schooling and are insisted on by most current testing systems are inadequate for a new, highly networked information age. Failure to help all students acquire literacies for this age will not serve them or society well. Not to teach the necessary skills, strategies, dispositions, and social practices is to deny children full access to economic, social, and political participation in the new global society. Not to assess these capabilities will result in curricular neglect and a lack of information to inform instruction.

The Learning of Language

By the time children arrive at school, they have learned to speak at least one language and have mastered most of the language structures they will ever use. Through social interaction, using the language they hear around them from birth, they have developed, without their awareness, the underlying rules of grammar and the vocabulary that give meaning to the world as they see it. Nonetheless, we often teach language in schools as if children came to our classrooms with little or no language competence. Nothing could be further from the truth. Children can request, demand, explain, recount, persuade, and express opinions. They bring to school the ability to narrate their own life histories. They are authors creating meaning with language long before they arrive at school.

As children acquire language in social interaction, particularly with others whose language is different or more complex, they gain flexibility in using language for different purposes and in different social situations. Learning a second language or dialect roughly parallels learning the first, for learning any language also entails becoming competent in the social relationships that underlie it. Children also develop fluent use of language without explicit knowledge of or instruction in rules and grammars. This means that grammars and rules are taught most productively as tools for analyzing language after it has been acquired. Even adults who have considerable facility with the language frequently can articulate few, if any, grammar or language rules. In spite of this truism, we often go about assessment and instruction in schools as if this were not the case.

Furthermore, although we pretend otherwise, language is not acquired in any simple hierarchical sequence.

In some ways, school actually plays a modest role in language acquisition, the bulk of which occurs outside of school. In schools, we must learn to teach language in a way that preserves and respects individuality at the same time that we empower students to learn how to be responsible and responsive members of learning communities. In other words, we must respect their right to their own interpretations of language, including the texts they read and hear, but we must help them learn that meaning is negotiated with other members of the learning communities within which they live and work. To participate in that negotiation, they must understand and be able to master the language practices and means of negotiation of the cultures within which they live. They must understand the language conventions that are sanctioned in different social situations and the consequences of adhering to or violating those conventions.

Although much of our language is learned outside school, studying language is the foundation of all schooling, not just of the language arts. For example, in science class, we make knowledge of the world using language. To study science, then, we must study the language through which we make scientific knowledge, language that has an important impact on the curriculum. If in reading and writing about science the language is dispassionate and distancing, then that is part of the knowledge that students construct about science, part of the way they relate to the world through science.

The Assessment of Language

Our description of language and language learning has important implications for the assessment of language, first because it is the object of assessment (the thing being assessed) and second because it is the medium of assessment (the means through and within which we assess). Instructional outcomes in the language arts and assessment policies and practices should reflect what we know about language and its acquisition. For example, to base a test on the assumption that there is a single correct way to write a persuasive essay is a dubious practice. Persuading someone to buy a house is not the same as persuading someone to go on a date. Persuading someone in a less powerful position is not the same as persuading someone in a more powerful position—which is to say that persuasive practices differ across situations, purposes, and cultural groups. Similarly, that texts can (and should) be read from different perspectives must be taken as a certainty—a goal of schooling not to be disrupted by assessment practices that pretend otherwise. To assert through a multiple-choice test that a piece of text has only one meaning is unacceptable, given what we know of language.

Moreover, to the extent that assessment practices legitimize only the meanings and language practices of particular cultural groups, these practices are acts of cultural oppression. When our assessments give greater status to one kind of writing over another—for example, expository writing over narrative writing—we are making very powerful controlling statements about the legitimacy of particular ways of representing the world. These statements tend to be reflected in classroom practices.

When we attempt to document students' language development, we are partly involved in producing that development. For example, if we decide that certain skills are "basic" and some are "higher level," and that the former need to be acquired before the latter, that decision affects the way we organize classrooms, plan our teaching, group students, and discuss reading and writing with them. The way we teach literacy, the way we sequence lessons, the way we group students, even the way we physically arrange the classroom all have an impact on their learning.

The Language of Assessment

Because it involves language, assessment is an interpretive process. Just as we construct meanings for texts that we read and write, so do we construct "readings" or interpretations of our students based upon the many "texts" they provide for us. These assessment texts come in the form of the pieces that students write, their responses to literature, the various assignments and projects they complete, the contributions they make to discussions, their behavior in different settings, the questions they ask in the classroom or in conferences, their performances or demonstrations involving language use, and tests of their language competence. Two different people assessing a student's reading or writing, his or her literate development, may use different words to describe it.

Standards for the Assessment of Reading and Writing

In classrooms, teachers assess students' writing and reading and make evaluative comments about writers whose work is read. The language of this classroom assessment becomes the language of the literate classroom community and thus becomes the language through which students evaluate their own reading and writing. If the language of classroom assessment implies that there are several interpretations of any particular text, students will come to gain confidence as they assess their own interpretations and will value diversity in the classroom. If, on the other hand, the language of classroom assessment implies that reading and writing can be reduced to a simple continuum of quality, students will assess their own literacy only in terms of their place on that continuum relative to other students, without reflecting productively on their own reading and writing practices.

When teachers write report cards, they are faced with difficult language decisions. They must find words to represent a student's literate development in all its complexity, often within severe time, space, and format constraints. They must also accomplish this within the diverse relationships and cultural backgrounds among the parents, students, and administrators who might read the reports. Some teachers are faced with reducing extensive and complex knowledge about each student's development to a single word or letter. This situation confronts them with very difficult ethical dilemmas. Indeed, the greater the knowledge the teacher has of the student's literacy, the more difficult this task becomes.

But it is not just classroom assessment that is interpretive. The public "reads" students, teachers, and schools from the data that are provided. Parents make sense of a test score or a report card grade or comment based on their own schooling history, beliefs, and values. A test score may look "scientific" and "objective," but it too must be interpreted, which is always a subjective and value-laden process.

The terms with which people discuss students' literacy development have also changed over time. For example, in recent history, students considered to be having difficulty becoming literate have acquired different labels, such as *basic writer, remedial reader, disadvantaged, learning disabled, underachiever, struggling student,* or *retarded reader.* These different terms can have quite different consequences. Students described as "learning disabled" are often treated and taught quite differently from students who are similarly literate but described as "remedial readers."

Further, assessment itself is the object of much discussion, and the language of that discussion is also important. For example, teachers' observations are often described as informal and subjective and contrasted with test results that are considered "formal" and "objective." The knowledge constructed in a discussion that uses these terms would be quite different from that constructed in a discussion in which teachers' observations were described as "direct documentation" and test results as "indirect estimation."

Assessment terms change as different groups appropriate them for different purposes and as situations change. Recent discussions about assessment have changed some of the ways in which previously reasonably predictable words are used, belying the simplicity of the glossary we include at the end of this document. For example, the term *norm-referenced* once meant that assessment data on one student, typically test data, were interpreted in comparison with the data on other students who were considered similar. A norm-referenced

Standards for the Assessment of Reading and Writing

interpretation of a student's writing might assert that it is "as good as that of 20 percent of the students that age in the country." Similarly, the term *criterion-referenced assessment* once meant simply that a student's performance was interpreted with respect to a particular level of performance—either it met the criterion or it did not. Recently, however, it has become much less clear how these terms are being used. The line between criterion and norm has broken down. For example, *criterion* has recently come to mean "dimension" or "valued characteristic." *Norm* has come to be used in much the same sense. But even in the earlier (and still more common) meaning, most criteria for criterion-referenced tests are arrived at by finding out how a group of students performs on the test and then setting criteria in accord with what seems a reasonable point for a student's passing or failing the test.

In other words, assessment is never merely a technical process. Assessment is always representational and interpretive because it involves representing children's development. Assessment practices shape the ways we see children, how they see themselves, and how they engage in future learning. Assessment is social and, because of its consequences, political. As with other such socially consequential practices, it is necessary to have standards against which practitioners can judge the responsibility of their practices.

Following are the summary paragraphs for all eleven standards. To read the expanded discussions and the case studies, see http://www.ncte.org/standards/assessmentstandards/introduction.

The Standards

1. The interests of the student are paramount in assessment.

Assessment experiences at all levels, whether formative or summative, have consequences for students (see standard 7). Assessments may alter their educational opportunities, increase or decrease their motivation to learn, elicit positive or negative feelings about themselves and others, and influence their understanding of what it means to be literate, educated, or successful. It is not enough for assessment to serve the well-being of students "on average"; we must aim for assessment to serve, not harm, each and every student.

2. The teacher is the most important agent of assessment.

Most educational assessment takes place in the classroom, as teachers and students interact with one another. Teachers design, assign, observe, collaborate in, and interpret the work of students in their classrooms. They assign meaning to interactions and evaluate the information that they receive and create in these settings. In short, teachers are the primary agents, not passive consumers, of assessment information. It is their ongoing, formative assessments that primarily influence students' learning. This standard acknowledges the critical role of the teacher and the consequences and responsibilities that accompany this role.

3. The primary purpose of assessment is to improve teaching and learning.

Assessment is used in educational settings for a variety of purposes, such as keeping track of learning, diagnosing reading and writing difficulties, determining eligibility for programs, evaluating programs, evaluating teaching, and reporting to others. Underlying all these purposes is a basic concern for improving teaching and learning. In the United States it is common to use testing for accountability, but the ultimate goal remains the improvement of teaching and learning. Similarly, we use assessments to determine eligibility for special education services, but the goal is more appropriate teaching and better learning for particular students. In both cases, if improved teaching and learning do not result, the assessment practices are not valid (see standard 7).

4. Assessment must reflect and allow for critical inquiry into curriculum and instruction.

Sound educational practices start with a curriculum that values complex literacy, instructional practices that nurture it, and assessments that fully reflect it. In order for assessment to allow productive inquiry into curriculum and instruction, it must reflect the complexity of that curriculum as well as the instructional practices in schools. This is particularly important because assessment shapes teaching, learning, and policy. Assessment that reflects an impoverished view of literacy will result in a diminished curriculum and distorted instruction and will not enable productive problem solving or instructional improvement. Because assessment shapes instruction, the higher the stakes of the assessment, the more important it is that it reflect this full complexity.

5. Assessment must recognize and reflect the intellectually and socially complex nature of reading and writing and the important roles of school, home, and society in literacy development.

Literacy is complex, social, and constantly changing. The literacies of students graduating from high school today were barely imaginable when they began their schooling. Outside of school, students live and will go on to work in a media culture with practices unlike those currently occurring in school (even in the setting of the school media center). Students need to acquire competencies with word processors, blogs, wikis, Web browsers, instant messaging, listservs, bulletin boards, virtual worlds, video editors, presentation software, and many other literate tools and practices. Traditional, simple definitions of literacy will not help prepare students for the literate lives of the present—let alone the future. Consequently, reading and writing cannot usefully be assessed as a set of isolated, independent tasks or events. It is critical to gather specific information about materials, tasks, and media being used with students for both instructional and assessment purposes. In addition, we need to assess how practices are used to participate in the broader media culture as well as to examine how the broader culture assigns status to some practices over others (e.g., texting as contrasted to writing paragraph summaries in language arts class).

Whatever the medium, literacy is social and involves negotiations among authors and readers around meanings, purposes, and contexts. Literate practices are now rarely solitary cognitive acts. Furthermore, literate practices differ across social and cultural contexts and across different media. Students' behavior in one setting may not be at all representative of their behavior in another. This may be particularly true of English-language learners who may lack the fluency to express themselves fully inside the classroom but may be lively contributors in their families and communities.

6. Assessment must be fair and equitable.

We live in a multicultural society with laws that promise equal rights to all. Our school communities must work to ensure that all students, as different as they are in cultural, ethnic, religious, linguistic, and economic background, receive a fair and equitable education. Assessment plays an important part in ensuring fairness and equity, first, because it is intimately related to curriculum, instruction, and learning, and second, because assessment provides a seemingly impartial way of determining who should and who should not be given access to educational institutions and resources. To be fair, then, assessment must be as free as possible of biases based on ethnic group, gender, nationality, religion, socioeconomic condition, sexual orientation, or disability. Furthermore, assessment must help us to confront biases that exist in schooling.

7. The consequences of an assessment procedure are the first and most important consideration in establishing the validity of the assessment.

Tests, checklists, observation schedules, and other assessments cannot be evaluated out of the context of their use. If a perfectly reliable and comprehensive literacy test were designed but using it took three weeks away from children's learning and half the annual budget for instructional materials, we would have to weigh these consequences against any value gained from using the test. If its use resulted in teachers building a productive learning community around the data and making important changes in their instruction, we would also have to weigh these consequences. This standard essentially argues for "environmental impact" projections, along with careful, ongoing analyses of the consequences of assessment practices. Responsibility for this standard lies with the entire school community, to ensure that assessments are not used in ways that have negative consequences for schools and students. Any assessment procedure that does not contribute positively to teaching and learning should not be used.

8. The assessment process should involve multiple perspectives and sources of data.

Perfect assessments and perfect assessors do not exist. Every person involved in assessment is limited in his or her interpretation of the teaching and learning of reading and writing. Similarly, each text and each assessment procedure has its own limitations and biases. Although we cannot totally eliminate these biases and limitations from people or tests, we can try to ensure that they are held in balance and that all stakeholders are made aware of them. The more consequential the decision, the more important it is to seek diverse perspectives and independent sources of data. For example, decisions about placement in or eligibility for specialized programs have a profound influence on a student's life and learning. Such decisions are simply too important to make on the basis of a single measure, evaluation tool, or perspective.

9. Assessment must be based in the local school learning community, including active and essential participation of families and community members.

Standards for the Assessment of Reading and Writing

The teacher is the primary agent of assessment and the classroom is the location of the most important assessment practices, but the most effective assessment unit is the local school learning community. First, the collective experience and values of the community can offer a sounding board for innovation and multiple perspectives to provide depth of understanding and to counter individual and cultural biases. Second, the involvement of all parties in assessment encourages a cooperative, committed relationship among them rather than an adversarial one. Third, because language learning is not restricted to what occurs in school, assessment must go beyond the school curriculum.

The local school learning community is also a more appropriate foundation for assessment than larger units such as the school district, county, state, province, or country. These larger units do not offer the relational possibilities and commitments necessary for a learning community. The distance from the problems to be solved and among the participants reduces the probability of feelings of involvement and commitment and increases the possibility that assessment will become merely a means of placing blame.

10. All stakeholders in the educational community—students, families, teachers, administrators, policymakers, and the public—must have an equal voice in the development, interpretation, and reporting of assessment information.

Each of the constituents named in this standard has a stake in assessment. Students are concerned because their literacy learning, their concepts of themselves as literate people, and the quality of their subsequent lives and careers are at stake. Teachers have at stake their understandings of their students, their professional practice and knowledge, their perceptions of themselves as teachers, and the quality of their work life and standing in the community. Families clearly have an investment in their children's learning, well-being, and educational future. The public invests money in education, in part as an investment in the future, and has a stake in maintaining the quality of that investment. The stewardship of the investment involves administrators and policymakers. Assessment is always value laden, and the ongoing participation of all parties involved in it is necessary in a democratic society. When any one perspective is missing, silenced, or privileged above others, the assessment picture is distorted.

11. Families must be involved as active, essential participants in the assessment process.

In many schools, families stand on the periphery of the school community, some feeling hopeless, helpless, and unwanted. However, the more families understand their children's progress in school, the more they can contribute to that progress. If teachers are to understand how best to assist children from cultures that are different from their own, families are a particularly important resource. Families must become, and be helped to become, active participants in the assessment process.

For the complete Standards *document, see http://www.ncte.org/standards/assessmentstandards/ introduction or https://secure.ncte.org/store/assessment-standards-revised.*

Teaching and Writing in a Brave New World: A Case for Teacher Leadership for Writing Assessment

In the past 30 years, research has produced revolutionary changes in our understanding of language, learning, and the complex literacy demands of our rapidly changing society.
—IRA–NCTE *Standards for the Assessment of Reading and Writing*, Rev. ed. (1)

How many goodly creatures are there here! How beauteous mankind is! O brave new world That has such people in't!
—Shakespeare, *The Tempest* (act 4, Scene 1)

The *Standards for the Assessment of Reading and Writing*, produced by the International Reading Association (IRA) and the National Council of Teachers of English (NCTE), make one thing perfectly clear: we teachers find ourselves in a brave new world. Research and experience over the past few decades have changed our fundamental conceptions of reading, writing, language, learning, assessment, and schooling:

- Once understood as discrete decoding and encoding skills, reading and writing are now understood as complex personal and social processes of meaning-making that take place over time and across a wide range of forms and media.

- Once conceived as a neutral tool for communicating information and ideas, language is now conceived as a cultural practice that mediates—indeed, constructs—our experience of reality.
- Once seen as the acquisition of transmitted knowledge, learning is now viewed as a contextualized, interactive process of inquiry.
- Once practiced only as a summative check on learning, assessment is now practiced as a highly contextualized, often communal, formative component of teaching and learning.
- Once charged with teaching the "3Rs," schools have become the primary caretaker of a complex multicultural and multilingual society, responsible for teaching not only "the basics" but also citizenship, life skills, creativity and innovation, character, information and media literacy, entrepreneurialism, sex education, global awareness, ethical responsibility, emotional intelligence, collaboration and teamwork, and much, much more.

Many of the concepts in this last laundry list fall under the heading "Twenty-First-Century Skills." There is widespread agreement that our historical moment, and in particular the proliferation of information and communication technologies, places special demands on literacy—or, more properly, litera*cies*. In its "Definition of 21st Century Literacies," for instance, NCTE claims that "a literate person" must now possess a range of "multiple, dynamic, and malleable" literacies that allow her or him to do the following:

- develop proficiency with the tools of technology
- build relationships with others to pose and solve problems collaboratively and cross-culturally
- design and share information for global communities to meet a variety of purposes
- manage, analyze, and synthesize multiple streams of simultaneous information
- create, critique, analyze, and evaluate multimedia texts
- attend to the ethical responsibilities required by these complex environments

Turning back to the IRA–NCTE *Standards for the Assessment of Reading and Writing* (SARW), we can see that these increasing and ever-changing literacy demands place special demands on teachers of reading and writing. According to the SARW,

> we must be concerned about the stances and practices involved in taking an idea presented in one modality (e.g., print) and transcribing or transmediating it into another (e.g., digital video), and we must consider what possibilities and limitations a particular mode offers and how that relates to its desirability over other modes for particular purposes and situations. (5)

Further, "[s]tudents need to acquire competencies with word processors, blogs, wikis, Web browsers, instant messaging, listservs, bulletin boards, virtual worlds, video editors, presentation software, and many other literate tools and practices" (18).

As if all this weren't enough to make us feel downright Miranda-like—untutored, unsure of what's in store, maybe even wide-eyed in amazement—the standards also place *assessment* in the hands of teachers. According to Standard 2, "The teacher is the most important agent of assessment" (13). Though the authors of the standards are careful to indicate that responsibility for assessment is shared among educational stakeholders, they insist that teachers play a leading role in shaping "communities of inquiry" in their schools and communities. In the end, they write, "as agents of assessment, teachers must take responsibility for making and sharing judgments about students' achievement and progress. They cannot defer to others or to other instruments" (14).

Brave new world indeed. Mention assessment and many teachers might be put in mind of that *other* "brave new world": Aldous Huxley's dystopian novel by that name. In Huxley's imagined world, a World State administers life to docile people who have been robbed of their identity and humanity through advances in biotechnology. We doubt most teachers' anxieties about assessment extend quite *that* far, but for many teachers, assessment is a technical practice they don't feel they understand very well, wielded by people with more power than they have (administrators, policymakers, the testing industry) in order to control their professional work. In this age of "accountability," teachers have been treated as targets of assessment rather than agents of it; assessment is something that is done to teachers, not something they do.

And now here come the SARW, adding assessment to teachers' already full plates. Why, we might reasonably ask, should we commit ourselves to this work that has so often been used by others to rank and sort our students, control our teaching, and punish our schools? And where will we find the time and energy for more work on top of everything else we're doing as the literacy ground shifts under our feet?

As a high school English language arts teacher (Eric) and a college writing teacher (Chris), we take these questions seriously. We know it is not self-evident that teachers should, or even can, take on the roles and responsibilities assigned to them by the SARW. We recognize that some teachers wish to reject this brave new world. Still, we're determined to join with the authors of the SARW and do our best to convince you that it is incumbent upon all teachers who have anything to do with student writing—and we hope that's most teachers!—to embrace writing assessment. We urge you not only to become "literate" in writing assessment, but also to develop expertise in it and even to provide leadership for it in your classroom, school, community, and perhaps beyond.

But this book is more than just an argument; it's also a resource devoted to helping you learn *how* to gain writing assessment literacy, develop writing assessment expertise, and practice writing assessment leadership. In keeping with the aims of the Principles in Practice imprint, we provide numerous illustrations drawn from classrooms and communities. Each chapter after this one provides a mix of discussion and examples of colleagues engaged in writing assessment as practitioners, experts, and leaders. We also point you to other resources to support you as you become the "agent of assessment" the SARW encourage you to be.

But if you are still wondering *why* you should invest your precious time and energy in this work—or perhaps how you can convince your colleagues to do so— we begin with our case for teacher leadership for writing assessment.

Our Case

Here is the crux of the case we want to make: *A brave new world of literacy is upon us. Teachers can either lead the way by helping our students navigate this exciting if sometimes perilous environment, or we can leave students to their own devices and those of "reformers" and their "experts" who may not understand teaching, learning, or writing—and certainly don't understand them in the intimate way teachers do.* The former is a daunting challenge but full of exciting opportunities; the latter would be disastrous for students, education, and our democracy.

If this framing of the case seems melodramatic, consider the following propositions, which we explore and defend in more detail in the following sections:

1. Young people today are writing more than ever before, and they will continue to do so—in many forums and media and with various consequences—whether their teachers are there to guide them or not. We must learn to read, assess, and respond to the diverse ways of writing they are inventing because this writing is both exciting and dangerous. As teachers, we must lead by helping to shape how our students value, participate in, and create the brave new world of writing in the twenty-first century.

2. Even as the means of writing production have been opened up to young people—if they have access to a computer and an Internet connection, they can publish their writing with a few clicks—most of them do not feel they have a *meaningful* and *consequential* public voice. Their writing outside of school, while *potentially* public, functions mostly (if paradoxically) as privatized public discourse. Meanwhile, their writing in school is often produced for the purpose of closed-circuit assessments (they write to be evaluated, not to be read). For all the unprecedented writing they are doing—much of it online—they have precious few public spaces available to them in which they can influence others, especially adult decision-makers. As teachers, we must lead by teaching and assess-

ing writing in ways that open up meaningful and consequential opportunities for young writers.

      3. Like young people, teachers have a difficult time gaining a meaningful and consequential public voice. Curriculum and instruction are largely and increasingly imposed on schools by policymakers and technical experts who are not themselves educators and who do not recognize or value local contexts of practice. Meanwhile, teachers are being made scapegoats of an underfunded public school system and are often cruelly vilified as incompetent public servants. As teachers, we must lead by teaching and assessing writing in ways that publicly proclaim and honor our professional judgment.

Now let's slow this down a bit. We begin with the brave new world that has opened up for (and is being opened up by) young writers.

Writing 2.0

We would like you to meet Chris's daughter Erin. Erin is a smart, spunky eleven-year-old who spent her first nine years in Nebraska and is now living with her parents and older sister near Boston. She is also a writer. To put a finer point on it, Erin is an almost obsessive self-sponsored writer. She composes poems, short stories, plays, songs, diary entries, letters, emails, PowerPoint presentations, podcasts, webpages, blog entries, iMovies, and more. She's also working on a science fiction novel and she is the publisher of her own independent newspaper, *The Town Herald* (circulation appx. 30). As you can see from this list, Erin is an avid and competent user of a wide range of writing technologies, including those we call "Web 2.0." These interactive technologies have allowed her to remain connected to her Nebraska friends via email, instant messaging, and video chatting (sometimes all of these at once). She uses the Internet to exchange photographs with these friends and she makes e-cards, slide shows, and home movies for them. Because she has access to computer technology and the (mostly self-taught) literacy abilities to use them effectively, she is able to communicate with and express herself using multiple modalities and in various media.

      To be sure, Erin is unusually prolific, and she is a child of considerable privilege. Still, the range and complexity of her literate life, and the increasing demands that will be placed on it as she nears and enters adulthood, are not altogether unusual. Consider, for instance, Kylene Beers's depiction in *Adolescent Literacy* of Collin, the failing, near-dropout high school student who ducks out of English class to work on his blog, on which he explores environmental issues (Beers, Probst, and Rief). Students nearly everywhere, as Kathleen Blake Yancey suggests,

> write words on paper, yes—but . . . also compose words and images and create audio files on Web logs (blogs), in word processors, with video editors and Web editors

and in e-mail and on presentation software and in instant messaging and on listservs and on bulletin boards—and no doubt in whatever genre will emerge in the next ten minutes. ("Made Not Only," 298)

Kids and adolescents are using Internet-enabled writing technologies to engage in a wide variety of collaborative activities, including—to choose just a few random examples—playing role-based games, writing fan fiction and making fan films, standing up to standardized testing, bullying peers into suicide, or supporting one another's quests to become or remain anorexic. Moreover, as NCTE's "Definition of 21st Century Literacies" suggests, and as numerous reports and vision statements on 21st century literacies confirm, new and emerging information and communication technologies entail ever-rising literacy demands. (See, for instance, NCTE's *21st Century Literacies: A Policy Research Brief*; The Partnership for 21st Century Skills website; and the Center for Media Literacy's "Literacy for the 21st Century.")

Again, brave new world. What's "new" about new media is that it allows virtually anyone not only to consume information and ideas but also to share and publish them (see Shirky). As a result, for better *and* for worse, young writers are not waiting for adults to provide forums for their writing; they are creating those forums for themselves. They are citizens of what Yancey calls an emerging "writing public," the defining feature of which is that *"no one is forcing [it] to write"* ("Made Not Only," 300; emphasis in original). In other words, this writing—like most of Erin's writing, or at least the writing that matters most to her—is taking place largely outside of school.

Does this mean teachers need to learn and teach every new communication and information technology that comes along? Absolutely not. We are not technology trainers. Nor does it mean that we should seek to replicate in our classrooms the kinds of new media composing that Erin and her peers are doing. Though certainly teachers are making excellent uses of Web 2.0 writing tools in their classrooms (see Herrington, Hodgson, and Moran, for example) and should continue to do so, the point is not to make classrooms mirror *other* literacy environments. In classrooms, we want students to do particular kinds of reading, writing, and thinking that we value, which may or may not be abundantly available to young people in other places. Our goal should be to help students value, reflect critically on, and practice their various literacies across multiple contexts.

What does this have to do with writing assessment? Everything, as it turns out. New ways to write and new kinds of writing require new ways of reading and evaluating. As teachers, we need to help students make sense of their expanding literacies and the texts and images they produce—and we need to make sense of these ourselves. To take a simple example, writers of Web-based texts do not build their credibility in the same ways that writers of print texts do; in fact, writers of

Web-based texts are often corporate or anonymous composers—compilers—of texts that are fragmented, associative, and often made up of texts or objects that already existed in other contexts. How can we help students think through issues of authorship, credibility, and source use and citation in these kinds of environments? What new kinds of criteria will we need to assess the value of these texts?

Even if we do not share all of our students' proliferating literacies, we can take advantage of them as we help our students write in meaningful and responsible ways in all facets of their lives. There is no question that our students will write, whether we tell them to or not. The only question is whether we will be there when they do, ready to be responsive conversation partners as they create their own brave new worlds with their words.

Privatized Public Writing

But there is a curious paradox about all this public writing: relatively little of it is meaningful and consequential in the adult world of decision-makers. Certainly few young people think so. The chief finding of the 2008 National Commission on Writing report *Writing, Technology and Teens* is that teens write a lot—almost constantly—but they do not consider much of this activity, especially the large portion of it they do online, as "real" writing. As the authors of the report write, "[t]he act of exchanging emails, instant messages, texts, and social network posts is communication that carries the same weight to teens as phone calls and between-class hallway greetings" (Lenhart, Arafeh, Smith, and Rankin Macgill i).

And no wonder: at the same time that many young people are "going public" with their writing, we are seeing public spaces for writing shrink and disappear. We realize this might sound like a strange claim in light of all we've said about the Internet and young people's proliferating literacies, but let's go back to Erin for a moment. It is clearly the case that Erin is growing up in a world of what cultural theorists call time–space compression (see Harvey). Her use of new media technologies has obliterated the time and space between the Midwest and the East Coast of the United States. But for all this frenetic communicative and expressive activity, it is essentially private. In all the forms of writing we've mentioned, Erin is writing only to people she knows about the same topics she would—and does—discuss with friends in person or in letters sent by post: weather, school, friends, books. Even her "newspaper," which treats a broader range of topics (politics, sports, advice, etc.), is written and read only by people she knows well about topics of mutual interest. Similarly, her webpages and blogs are not public to anyone she does not invite to view them. All of this wonderful writing is enormously meaningful to her and to those of us lucky enough to read it, but it is not in any meaningful sense "public" writing.[1]

Of course, some young people *are* using electronic communication and information technologies in publicly consequential ways, as some of our previous examples—the antitesting activists, the "pro-ana" (anorexia advocates)—suggest. But these are the rare exceptions. For most young people, their online writing is only nominally "public"; it doesn't function in any meaningful way *as* public writing.[2] Some of this writing may happen in public, but even then, like many phone calls and hallway greetings (or gossip), it is engaged as a private exchange without a public dimension. Of course, it is possible that virtually anyone *could* listen in on online conversations, as we rightly warn young people. But the stories about Internet predators and prospective employers learning embarrassing things about would-be employees are exceptions that prove the rule: almost all the time, almost all the so-called public writing on the Internet has no audience beyond a very limited affinity group. What these stories really demonstrate is just how private that writing is intended to be: the concern here—reasonably enough—is that people will inadvertently reveal compromising information about their *private* lives.

Our culture might offer young people free blogging tools and Twitter accounts, but it doesn't provide even the most privileged among them with forums in which to deliberate, formulate considered opinions, and weigh in on matters of public significance. As teachers interested in public writing quickly come to learn, there are few venues to which a student of any age can send her writing with the realistic expectation that serious adults in positions of power are likely to read it and deliberate over its ideas. Many of us have helped our own students laboriously design websites that get only a handful of hits, Facebook groups that collect only a few members, and blogs that garner only a comment or two (usually from a friend).

Strangely, even as information and communication technologies proliferate, the public sphere is actually getting smaller, thanks to the privatization of so much of what used to be public space—public lands, public bandwidth, community airwaves—not to mention the overwhelmingly swift and comprehensive consolidation of corporate media outlets (see Welch). Instead of engaging in robust public deliberation, we have created a culture—at least hinting at Huxley's imagined administered world—in which most important decisions are made by those who own these previously public resources and their bands of "experts": people with specialized, often technical, knowledge. This culture leaves little room for ordinary people, including most young people, to write in ways that are likely to affect decision-makers. Part of what it means to be there for our students as writers in this brave new world, then, is to help them create public spaces *for* their writing and *with* their writing.

Privatized Teaching

But teachers will not be able to help create public spaces for students unless we also create public spaces for our own work—because teaching, too, has become privatized. As Michelle Comstock, Mary Ann Cain, and Lil Brannon suggest, "with regards to teachers of writing, privatization is also about privatizing expertise and decision-making so that the people who are most impacted by such policies are permitted no place and no authority to speak on their own behalf" (9). In other words, important educational decisions are rarely made by those who actually spend their days in classrooms; instead, they are made by "experts" remote from scenes of instruction.

Given our focus on assessment in this book, it is important to recognize that standardized testing has played a major role in the privatization of teaching. It has been used as a tool by policymakers and the testing industry to control curriculum and instruction from outside of schools (as we hear so often, "what we test is what we teach"). It has provided fodder for continuous, manufactured educational crises, which propagate the idea that teachers (unlike "objective" measurement experts) cannot be trusted (see Berliner and Biddle). It has put schools in competition with one another, much as businesses are put in competition in private-sector markets. And it has brought an army of private vendors—test and textbook makers, off-the-shelf curriculum providers, test-prep companies, purveyors of a wide range of "supplemental services"—into the schools.

Though the Bush-era No Child Left Behind law is widely credited with (or decried for) underwriting these developments—and surely it did—recent policy developments promise to remove teachers even further from educational decision making. The Common Core State Standards Initiative (CCSSI), coordinated by the National Governors Association (NGA) and the Council of Chief State School Officers (CCSSO), is an effort to provide a single set of standards for the nation (though it is adopted by individual states—forty-five, at last count). According to the initiative's mission statement, the purpose of the CCSSI is to "provide a consistent, clear understanding of what students are expected to learn, so teachers and parents know what they need to do to help them" (Common Core State Standards Initiative). Notice that teachers are the *targets* of the standards, not their originators: the standards "provide" them with "understanding." We can argue the pros and cons of the standards themselves, the very idea of national standards, and the heavy-handed way the federal government is ensuring states adopt them (by tying Race to the Top funding to their adoption by states). But what seems incontrovertible is that the process used to develop the standards was top-down and largely excluded teachers.

The English Language Arts Work Group for the CCSSI, for instance, consisted of fourteen members, ten of whom were associated with ACT, Achieve, or the College Board (these members had titles such as Senior Test Development Associate; Assistant Vice President, Educational Planning and Assessment System Development, Education Division; and Senior Director, Standards and Curriculum Alignment Services). The group also included representatives of three companies: America's Choice (an educational "solutions provider" owned by Pearson); Student Achievement Partners, LLC; and VockleyLang, LLC (a marketing firm). Rounding out the group was a lone retired English professor, well known for her work on the National Assessment of Educational Progress. Exactly zero practicing teachers served on this work group.

Meanwhile, teachers' professional organizations such as NCTE were relegated to the sidelines. As NCTE President Kylene Beers repeatedly reminded members of the organization in a series of open letters, NCTE's role was that of "independent critic." "NCTE was not invited to help author or provide feedback as standards were formulated," Beers noted in her letter of September 21, 2009, "however, in July, NCTE was invited to provide a response to [the first drafts of the standards]." NCTE assembled a Review Team that issued responses, which by all accounts were taken seriously by the NGA and CCSSO. But the fact remains that NCTE was invited only to *respond*; it was not a major player in the CCSSI. Instead of turning to professional organizations and classroom experts who spend their days with children, the NGA and CCSSO turned primarily to the private sector, recruiting high-ranking employees and managers in education "solutions" organizations and companies to create curricular standards.

Predictably, we are now seeing the emergence of a marketplace for curriculum and instruction professional development tools and "scalable educational technology solutions" based on the Common Core standards. The Gates Foundation and Pearson Foundation recently announced "a partnership aimed at crafting complete, online curricula for those standards in mathematics and English/language arts that span nearly every year of a child's precollegiate education" (Gewertz, "Gates"). (The Gates foundation has also awarded the Association for Supervision and Curriculum Development [ASCD] $3 million to promote the Common Core State Standards among teachers and contributed to the $7 million awarded to technology programs related to the Common Core standards by the Next Generation Learning Challenges initiative; see Nagel.) They will develop twenty-four courses, four of which will be available online for free, with the whole suite available for purchase—presumably from Pearson, the for-profit international media, publishing, and test-making corporation that operates the Pearson Foundation. While critics worry about the prospect of turning the nation's curriculum over to rich individuals and for-profit "entrepreneurs," the Obama administration apparently

welcomes this development. Here, for instance, is US Secretary of Education Arne
Duncan's Chief of Staff, Joann Weiss:

> The development of common standards and shared assessments radically alters the
> market for innovation in curriculum development, professional development, and for-
> mative assessments. Previously, these markets operated on a state-by-state basis, and
> often on a district-by-district basis. But the adoption of common standards and shared
> assessments means that education entrepreneurs will enjoy national markets where the
> best products can be taken to scale.

Meanwhile, two consortia are designing common assessment systems based
on the Common Core State Standards. Because these consortia will be enormously
important in the years to come, it is worth considering how they have operated
thus far. Allocated $350 million in Race to the Top funds, the consortia—the
Partnership for Assessment of Readiness for College and Careers (PARCC) and
the Smarter Balanced Assessment Consortium (SBAC)—represent all but a handful
of states and the District of Columbia. In a white paper titled "Designing Common
State Assessment Systems," the NGA and CCSSO explain that these consortia
are charged with designing "one or two" summative tests. (It is implied that the
organizations would have preferred one consortium, but the states could not come
to consensus on a single vision; for now, the organizations are settling for two, with
the hope that they will merge in the future.)

PARCC, as its name implies, is focused on preparing students for college and
work and on creating a streamlined, cost-effective system. SBAC includes emphases on professional development for and participation by teachers and computer-
assisted assessment.[3] But both consortia, like the CCSSI, are top-down efforts
devoted to designing educational programs *for* teachers and students. The PARCC
governance structure, described in the white paper, and the SBAC organizational
chart, provided on its website, are heavily skewed toward policymakers, state officials, and private technical and management partners. The PARCC governance
structure doesn't mention teachers at all; the SBAC organizational chart includes
"educator professional organizations" among a set of nine stakeholder groups at
the very bottom of the hierarchy.

So teachers are being removed further and further from their central location
in education, and assessment—standardized testing, in particular—is the primary
means of this displacement. Comstock and her colleagues urge writing teachers to
claim and create public space in and beyond our classrooms. They warn that
"[w]ithout adequate representation of their expertise in the decision-making process of schooling, the public spaces available for teachers and students to speak will
continue to shrink until the remaining public spaces become indistinguishable from
the private interests that seek to dominate and control public space" (5). We agree.

Our Better Judgment

We hope to have convinced you that there is too much at stake for teachers *not* to assert our leadership in this brave new world of literacy. We hope you share our belief that teachers need to work together to help create public spaces for writing and teaching.

But teacher leadership for writing assessment need not be only a defensive gesture: we believe teachers have much to gain by moving writing assessment to the center of our professional practice. Consider again our earlier point about how notions of credibility are changing in a new media landscape. One of the questions we asked was, "What new criteria will we need to assess the value of these texts?" As this question suggests, assessment is rooted in *values*. Any serious exercise in educational assessment focuses our attention on "what we really value" (Broad). It allows us to clarify our goals and to align our practices with those goals. And it allows us to hone our individual and collective judgment, which is the very lifeblood of our profession.

Why is teachers' professional judgment so important? *Judgment* has a few relevant meanings. In everyday parlance, it is an evaluation based on information or evidence. Clearly, teachers make judgments all the time, every day—about which activities to engage students in, about whether to challenge an unruly student on his behavior or let it go for now, about whether to review or move on to new material, about when a class is ready for an assessment . . . the list goes on. Second, in legal terminology, a judgment is a finding: a result, a decision. In law as in education, the best and most reliable judgments are those informed by intimate knowledge of a situation and its participants. And those who have extended, sustained experience in a field and are able to reflect on and learn from it are said to have judgment in the third sense: discernment, wisdom. Good judgment is earned through understanding situations in which decisions have impact: *to discern* means to see, recognize, comprehend. Wisdom and discernment are always rooted in shared values, forged by experience, and informed by inquiry.

Because we are *inside* the teaching and learning relationship with students on a daily basis, teachers' best judgment is shaped by shared school values, experiences with students and fellow teachers, and inquiry into teaching and learning. Unfortunately, some proponents of standardized tests believe they can do an end-run around this messy business about values, experience, and inquiry. But any serious person will conclude that these are not hindrances to meaningful education; they are its beating heart. They are also the heart of a functioning democracy, which requires careful, public deliberation. It is no coincidence that the citizens of Huxley's World Government are stripped of their ability for individual and collective judgment; without that, they are susceptible to being controlled by others.

What we're calling "our better judgment" is not a natural result of being placed in a classroom. Our judgment is only better than that of outsiders if it is informed by active and critical *inquiry* into reading, writing, language, learning, assessment, and schooling. Inquiry, as the authors of the SARW suggest, is both a problem-posing and a problem-solving activity that anchors effective assessment. The defining feature of any profession is that it inquires into and assesses its own values, procedures, and practices, and teaching is certainly no exception. If we are not inquiring into and assessing our work and the work of our students, we might be instructing, but we are not truly teaching. This is why teachers should embrace assessment-as-inquiry as a core, indispensable part of their daily work and their profession.

Yes, We Can

But even if teachers' professional judgment *should* be at the center of education, can we pull it off? *Can* teachers take the assessment reins and lead into the twenty-first century, considering our already busy, sometimes overwhelming, professional lives?

This book answers, resoundingly, *Yes, we can*. Why? Because assessment-as-inquiry—an idea offered by the SARW and elaborated throughout this book—is not something we do *in addition to* our work as teachers; it is an integral part of that work. To be sure, assessment has some technical dimensions, and we need to learn about them. But assessment is fundamentally a part of teaching and learning and thus falls well within our professional purview. In fact, because it helps us articulate our values and make sense of and coordinate the various components of our practice, assessment-as-inquiry has the potential to make our work easier, more manageable. We know that effective formative classroom assessments lead to significant learning gains for students, especially those who are "at risk" (Black and Wiliam; Guskey; Hughes; Wiliam). We're just coming to understand how assessment-as-inquiry supports *teacher* learning as well. We've also just begun learning how assessment can help teachers to inspect our own and our communities' values, to (re)invigorate our commitment to our work, and to help us gain more control over our profession.

But we won't ask you to take our word for it. Instead, in the chapters to follow, we introduce you to many of your colleagues who are using assessment in just these ways. We answer the "how" question by showing you how practicing teachers are doing the work of writing assessment.

One final word about the arc of this book. Chapter 2, on writing assessment literacy, is designed to help you understand and use writing assessment in your own classroom. Chapter 3, on writing assessment expertise, is designed to help you participate as a knowledgeable professional in your school's assessment activities. Chapter 4, on writing assessment leadership, is designed to help you shape assessment cultures and policies in your schools, districts, communities, and perhaps beyond. At each point in this arc, we imagine your assessment knowledge becoming deeper and its sphere of influence becoming broader. Of course, we recognize the dangers of appearing to lay out a rigid, linear trajectory comprising seemingly mutually exclusive categories. Our intent in proposing the arc is not didactic, but rather explanatory: we think it offers a useful way to describe various orientations and roles teachers take vis-à-vis assessment. We recognize that all teachers must work with and within the affordances and constraints of their situations. We all must begin where we are and do what we can. That said, it would be disingenuous to suggest that our goal with this book is anything less than helping *all* teachers— yes, including you!—to become assessment leaders.

Notes

1. As this book goes to press, Erin, motivated in part by the Occupy movement, has embarked on a new, public blog project—while still taking the necessary precautions, under her parents' watchful eyes, to protect her privacy—in which she takes on a range of political issues, from digital piracy legislation to transgender rights. She is slowly gaining more readers, including some strangers.

2. While some media and communications experts hail a new age of public participation (Shirky; Warnick), others suggest the digital "public sphere" harbors *anti*-social tendencies and lacks "clear frameworks of social obligation and political responsibility" (Keren 16).

3. SBAC's narrow definition of *assessment literate* teachers is telling; according to the SBAC website, these teachers have gotten "inside" the Common Core State Standards, have taught and measured them, and have learned how to intervene in students' learning if they have not mastered the standards.

Gaining Writing Assessment Literacy

[I]n order to (re)articulate assessment as something controlled by teachers to promote teaching and learning, teachers must learn not to avoid it or to leave it in the hands of professional testers or administrators.

—Brian Huot, *(Re)Articulating Writing Assessment for Teaching and Learning* (191)

An inquiry framework changes the role of assessment and the roles of the participants. Within this framework, assessment is the exploration of how the educational environment and the participants in the educational community support the process of students as they learn to become independent and collaborative thinkers and problem solvers.

—IRA–NCTE *Standards for the Assessment of Reading and Writing* (2)

T hey were some of the best teachers of writing we knew: engaged, reflective, knowledgeable professionals. We reached out to them because we knew they would have a lot to say about the topic of the book we were working on: writing assessment. We had much to learn from them—and much to share with our readers.

But then, this:

Chris/Eric: Tell us about your approach to teaching writing.

Teacher: Well, I think it's important for kids to have a real audience for their writing. So last year, we partnered with the historical society, and the kids researched the history of some of the important older buildings in the city. They produced a collection of mini-histories that are now part of the historical society archives. At the end of the year, they made oral presentations of their histories at a special community event hosted by the society. I've never seen kids so excited, and I think it's because they had a real audience for their writing and presentations. The community members, parents, and officers of the society were impressed by the depth of the kids' research and their poise as speakers. It was a great project, and I can't wait to do it again this year.

Chris/Eric: Sounds exciting. So how did you assess the writing?

Teacher: Oh . . . [*pause*] . . . we used a rubric—basically the 6 traits rubric. The history teacher graded the content and we English teachers graded the writing.

Again and again, our early conversations with colleagues followed the same pattern: great excitement about interesting, innovative writing projects and then, when the conversation turned to assessment . . . rubrics, rubrics, rubrics.

We understood, of course, that rubrics were an important and pervasive feature of the educational landscape. So it was not surprising to us that rubrics came up. What *was* surprising, at least at first, was that they were virtually *all* that came up.

But we knew there was much more to these teachers' assessment practices than rubrics. Surely, if assessment matters at all—and experience and research told us it does—then these teachers must have been doing more than merely applying off-the-shelf rubrics at the end of writing projects.

Thankfully, we were right. As it turned out, these teachers went far beyond rubrics. As we'll see in this chapter and those to follow, they engaged in writing assessment as a process of inquiry, as the framers of the IRA–NCTE *Standards for the Assessment of Reading and Writing* (SARW) discuss in their introduction and state in Standard 4 ("Assessment must reflect and allow for critical inquiry into curriculum and instruction" [16]). But interestingly, they did not think of this work as writing assessment. For them—and this is true for many teachers—writing *rubrics* had come to stand in for writing *assessment*.

There is, we acknowledge, something to be celebrated here. In the not-so-distant past, writing *tests* stood in for writing assessment. These tests were often "indirect" measures of writing: they didn't ask students to write at all, but instead quizzed them on usage, asked them to fill in correct verb forms, required them to select the sentence with the incorrect punctuation, etc. It wasn't until the 1970s that English teachers' arguments about the necessity of using actual student writing in large-scale assessments gained significant traction (see Elliot; White; Yancey, "Looking Back"). Even today, we continue to see so-called writing assessments that test students' descriptive knowledge of language conventions rather than their ability to write. But as the ubiquity of rubrics suggests, direct writing assessment is now a widely accepted practice.

Still, if direct writing assessment is a step forward, the conflation of writing assessment with rubrics is at least a half-step backward. This is not because rubrics are intrinsically bad; as we argue elsewhere, they are a tool that can be used effectively or ineffectively (Turley and Gallagher). Rather, the problem is that they too often become the be-all and end-all of assessment. This is like saying that a violin is the be-all and end-all of music. Even if you adore violins, you should be able to admit two things: there are bad ways to play violins, and violins are not the only way to make music.

Consider all that goes wrong in this way of thinking. If you're so crazy about violins that any old noise produced by one is, well, music to your ears, you'll never be able to help others appreciate violins. You're utterly undiscerning, unable to distinguish and describe the qualities of violin music—or violin noise. Meanwhile, you're missing out on the vast world of music not created by violins. In fact, we might say that you don't really know what music is if you listen only to violins.

This analogy might seem like a stretch. Music is a vast, multifarious art; writing assessment is a narrow, relatively straightforward educational practice. But one of our goals in this chapter, and throughout this book, is to show that writing assessment, too, is vast and multifarious—not at all a narrow technical practice.

Writing Assessment Defined

So what is *writing assessment*? We define it as "the process of gathering, analyzing, and using information about student writing for the purpose of supporting students as writers, informing writing instruction/curriculum/professional development, and/or making decisions about students as writers (proficiency, placement, promotion, etc.)." We rely on this definition throughout the book, but we want to note several of its features at the outset.

First, the phrase "the process of gathering, analyzing, and using information" should sound familiar: this is the inquiry process described in the SARW. According to the authors of the SARW, inquiry—unlike the traditional model of knowledge transmission—"values the ability to recognize problems and to generate multiple and diverse perspectives in trying to solve them" (2). Assessment-as-inquiry, we would add, is also about *formulating* questions and problems in meaningful and appropriate ways. It begins with framing relevant, useful questions. Then it asks us to engage various relevant answers to those questions as we hone our own professional judgment.

Second, according to our definition, writing assessment need not result in a grade, a score, or in fact any final evaluative judgment. A teacher who collects a set of student drafts, responds to them, and builds a lesson based on what she's read is engaging in writing assessment even if she doesn't grade or score that writing. "The primary purpose of assessment," according to Standard 3 of the SARW, "is to improve teaching and learning," not to produce scores or grades (15). Our hypothetical teacher is using the information she gathered both to support students as writers and to inform her writing instruction. In assessment language, this is a type of *formative* assessment because it is carried out *during* the teaching and learning process to support further learning. On the other hand, our definition also covers *summative* assessment, which is carried out *after* teaching and learning have occurred in order to evaluate, and typically categorize, what a student has learned at that point in time (by assigning it a value such as A, B, C, D, F; or 4, 3, 2, 1; or "advanced," "proficient," "progressing," "beginning").

Third, our definition is broad enough to encompass several "units of analysis." By this, we mean that we could analyze the work of a single student, or that of a class or a single teacher, or that of a program, school, district, state, or even larger grouping. We design assessments in ways that reveal information about what we want to know. And we design assessments to support our educational goals; as Standard 7 of the SARW states, "The consequences of an assessment procedure are the first and most important consideration in establishing the validity of the assessment" (22). As assessors, we ask: What do we want to learn? What do we want to *do* with what we learn?

Finally, notice that the various uses of the collected information in our definition all involve student *writing* and students as *writers*. This might seem obvious, but assessments often make use of student writing without being writing assessments. If we use students' lab reports solely to determine whether they understand a particular scientific concept or process, for instance, we are not engaged in writing assessment, even though students' writing abilities affect their performance on the assessment. For an assessment to be a *writing* assessment, the information must be analyzed and used in a way that addresses student writing and/or students as writers.

Despite this last proviso, our definition of writing assessment is purposely broad. As we will discuss later, one can use various tools and methods to *gather*, *analyze*, and *use* information about student writing. Rubrics are only one of these.

A (Cautionary) Note on "Formative" Assessments

One of the unfortunate features of the test-based accountability movement of the past two decades is its un-relenting, narrow emphasis on summative assessments. Because educational accountability is premised on comparability and competition, and because testing costs money, assessment policies tend to promote simple, cost-efficient, summative standardized tests. Meanwhile, formative assessments have been pushed aside. This development is especially unfortunate in light of recent evidence that rich, classroom-based formative assess-ments have significant positive effects on learning (especially for students who traditionally struggle in school), as well as evidence that summative assessments have negligible and sometimes even negative impacts on learn-ing (Andrade and Cizek; Black and Wiliam; Black et al., *Assessment*, "Working"; FairTest.com; Guskey; Hughes; Wiliam).

Perhaps even more distressing, though, are recent attempts by some testing and textbook companies to capital-ize (literally) on the findings about formative assessment by offering off-the-shelf "formative assessments." Often, these assessments are keyed to publishers' textbooks and are more like "interim" assessments or mini-summative assessments designed to predict how students will perform on a future summative assessment. Observers worry that the consortia currently designing assessments keyed to the Common Core State Standards (see Chapter 1) are planning to provide "formative" assessments (renamed "through-course assessments") that function in precisely this way (Gewertz, "Expert"). This is not formative assessment. Meaningful formative assessment of the sort research has proven to be effective is classroom based and teacher designed. As James Popham writes, "The closer that formative assessments are to the actual instructional events taking place in classrooms, the more likely will be their positive impact on student learning" ("Defining" 8). As teachers, we should not allow formative as-sessments to be hijacked by testing and textbook companies or the common-assessments consortia; we should devote ourselves to learning about, designing, and implementing regular, high-quality formative assessments *for* student learning (see also Krashen).

As violins are to music, rubrics can be an important instrument of writing assess-ment. But not always. And the contribution is not always salutary; sometimes it can be counterproductive—like a slow, poorly played violin solo in the middle of a driving rock song.

Still, we understand that rubrics are pervasive in schools today, and we also understand that the decision about whether to use them is not always left to teach-ers. So before exploring other ways to gather, analyze, and use information about student writing, it seems wise to start with this one.

As we explore rubrics, we want to emphasize that no rubric is ever going to *perform* assessment; people do, with or without rubrics. The question for teachers who work with rubrics, then, is *how* they can do so, thoughtfully and intentionally, understanding how rubrics fit into a broader approach to teaching and assessing writing. Our colleague Ryan Redmond[1] helps us think about this question.

Ryan Wrestles with Rubrics: Using Assessment to Talk with Students about Writing

As a middle school English and history teacher in Massachusetts and as a supervisor of placements and professional development at Tufts University, Ryan is simultaneously leery of and drawn to rubrics. He has read Peter Taubman's *Teaching by Numbers*, and he worries, along with Taubman, that "[w]hat is lost in . . . reliance on numerical data and its translation is the complexity and variety of experiences it purports to capture" (90). Similarly, he has read Maja Wilson's *Rethinking Rubrics in Writing Assessment*, and he agrees with her that one cannot capture what Ryan calls "the messy, beautiful twists and turns that can make writing powerful and

> **I think that it's possible—and necessary—to pay close, diligent attention to standards and quantifiable data and still create a classroom environment where learning involves and encourages complexity and messiness.**
>
> **—Ryan Redmond**

interesting" by filling in boxes and grids. At the same time, Ryan thinks "it's possible—and necessary—to pay close, diligent attention to standards and quantifiable data and still create a classroom environment where learning involves and encourages complexity and messiness." As he has worked and reworked rubrics with his colleagues and students, Ryan has come to see that they can be tools for sponsoring meaningful conversations about writing. In particular, Ryan believes rubrics have the potential to help students and teachers develop their capacity for making informed judgments about pieces of writing.

But Ryan is quick to add,

> A rubric is worth little if it is not accompanied by the following activities: analysis of writing samples; practice using rubrics to evaluate those samples; sharing and discussion of examples of the writing assignment at hand; peer sharing and review; revision; and written and verbal feedback from the teacher. All of these activities add richness, complexity, context, and definition to the simplistic, vague language of the rubric.

For Ryan, rubrics are useful if they provide shared language as a starting point for conversations about writing. They should not *become* that conversation or stand in its place.

Consider how Ryan worked with writing rubrics in his eighth-grade humanities classroom. Using as a point of departure Charles Wilson and Eric Schlosser's *Chew on This*—a book that, like Schlosser's *Fast Food Nation*, exposes the public

health issues in and inhumane treatment of animals by the fast food industry—
Ryan asked his students to compose what he called a "diary as an eater," a week-
long series of daily journal entries. At the beginning of this project, Ryan provided
students with three documents: an assignment sheet that listed the expectations
(number and length of entries), a rubric outlining the elements that would be
graded, and an example of his own diary.

The criteria on the 4-point rubric were fairly conventional: Ideas, Sentence
Fluency, Word Choice, and Conventions. But Ryan had taken care to write the
performance descriptors in student-friendly language. For instance, the 4 in the
Word Choice category read: "You use many strong, powerful words in each paragraph. You use lively vocabulary that really brings the writing to life," whereas the
1 in that category read: "You use very ordinary, dead words, and you tend to repeat
yourself." As Ryan points out,

> The terms *strong, powerful, ordinary,* and *dead* all require definition and specificity.
> Alone, they mean very little. In context and through conversation, they take shape.
> The work of the year for the class was to come to a clearer understanding and defini-
> tion of just what strong, powerful, and lively language was and how it could be put to
> effective use.

For example, Ryan had his students look carefully at the sample open-response
writing published by the Massachusetts Department of Elementary & Secondary Education (DESE) website. The class discussed the responses and assigned
them scores based on the DESE rubric. Only then did Ryan reveal the score the
response had received, at which point the class continued to debate and discuss the
merits and demerits of the writing. The point here, Ryan insists, is not "accura-
cy"—though he wants his students to know how the test scorers value writing—but
rather discussion, debate, and judgment about writing:

> The language of the rubrics is important, and I wanted my students to understand
> how to navigate that language and those documents, but in so doing, it was always my
> goal to draw connections between the limited language of the rubric and the expan-
> sive discussion about what makes writing worth reading. In these discussions, when
> my students moved from a DESE open-response example to an example from a book
> that we had read or were reading, I knew that the rubric was serving to give ground
> to and frame the discussion but not, in any way, to limit that discussion. I recall with
> great clarity, for instance, a spirited discussion among my students about styles of
> language used in Orwell's *Animal Farm* versus Golding's *Lord of the Flies.* My students
> were able to understand the impact of how writing is constructed when they discussed
> "style" within the context of a couple of brilliant, narrative-heavy pieces of literature.

Ryan also asked his students to discuss his own writing sample:

Day 2. Tuesday

I woke up a bit late this morning and therefore had to rush. My shower was shorter
than usual. I hastily got dressed and misbuttoned my shirt. I'm lucky that I didn't
dribble toothpaste everywhere. On the way out the door, in a flurry, I grabbed a ba-
nana to eat as I walked to work. I ate it so quickly that I barely tasted it. This, I know,
is not the way to eat breakfast. Morning is for slowly waking up and slowly getting
settled into the day. And eating a leisurely breakfast is all part of that. Unfortunately,
it felt like hyper-fast food.

Day 3. Wednesday

I woke up early this morning, thanks to getting to bed early the night before. I fell
asleep reading. At about three in the morning, I woke up with the light on and my
book—*The Colossus of New York* by Colson Whitehead—beneath my head. I turned
the light off, put the book on the floor and fell back asleep. Because I woke up so
early and felt so alert when I did so, I decided to make some toast and eggs, things I
usually only eat on the weekends. I toasted the slice of sourdough bread in a cast iron
pan on the stove, as I have no toaster. I cooked the egg over easy, the way that I like
them best. I finally sat down at my kitchen table, turned on some music, and—with
some hot sauce drizzled on top—ate my toast and egg. Unlike yesterday, today's
breakfast felt like slow food.

Ryan explains that sharing his own writing is an important part of this teaching:

[Students] were able to hear me talk about my own writing process—important modeling for them as writers. They were able to see the way that I took a journal about
meals and expanded it to include wider observations of moments in life. They were
able to brainstorm and discuss as a class what they did or did not like about the subject
matter, the sentence structure, and the word choices. They were able to debate,
grounded in the text at hand, where they would evaluate the writing on the various
elements of the rubric; for example, they were able to speak with increasing specificity
about what made language "powerful," "ordinary," or "dead." One conclusion that we
arrived at was that powerful language is that which surprises. By reading and analyzing and writing—and by sharing that writing—my students continued to develop
their ear for writing that felt common, tired, or predictable, and that which makes you
smile and nod and want more.

Then students began composing their own eating diaries. They frequently
brought their writing to class and exchanged their work for peer review, using the
rubric, written comments, and follow-up conversation. Ryan believes that putting
young writers in conversation with each other is crucial because "the audience that
students offer one another is different in kind" from the one a teacher can offer.
He says students' excitement about reading each other's entries was palpable.

"What is writing for," he asks, "if not for the sharing of ideas and glimpses of insight that it allows into one another?" Students then revised their writing based on conversations with and suggestions from peers and handed in their final drafts. Ryan read, commented on, and evaluated the work with the rubric before handing the work back to the students. Here are two examples of student entries:

> Tuesday, December 1: It is my birthday, so I got to pick where we ate. I chose Pellino's, an Italian restaurant in Marblehead. When we got there, I ordered a chicken parmigiana. It came out of the kitchen, warm and filling. The chicken was breaded, and not overcooked. The thin angel hair pasta was ideal: not too hard, but not too soft. For dessert, I audaciously ordered the legendary lava cake, and it was the most delectable dessert ever. The melted chocolate flowed out of the cake when I took the first bite. It was also served with ice cream, and velvety whipped cream. But my favorite part was the mint leaf. I love the fresh taste of mint after something so rich and thick.
>
> —Megan

> Day 1: It is my third week being a vegetarian. I made this choice after reading the chapter "Meat" in <u>Chew on This</u>. It told me about the way animals are treated in factory farms. After learning where my food came from, it became impossible to eat, so I gave up chicken, pork, and beef. I will continue to eat fish, eggs, and dairy products. One would think that the hardest part of this would be obvious: giving up meat. For me, it's having a family of carnivores. They question me routinely about not having steak, and what I'm going to eat while we're on vacation when they're all eating bacon. My parents don't believe me when I say I can cook for myself and let them eat what they want, so for dinner tonight, again, we're having fish.
>
> —Sasha

It is not difficult to see how writing such as this can occasion further discussion about textual matters such as word choice, process matters such as descriptive strategies, and what Ryan calls "life matters" such as ideas and beliefs. Ryan's rule about rubrics is simple: If they get in the way of discussions like these, they should not be used; if they help sponsor them, they can be part of a comprehensive approach to the teaching and talking about writing.

Assessment Literacy in an Inquiry Framework

Teachers reasonably disagree about the usefulness and appropriateness of rubrics; our goal here is not to reenter what we have called the Great Rubric Debate (Turley and Gallagher). Rather, we are interested in putting rubrics in perspective by showing how assessment-literate teachers such as Ryan *think about* and *use* rubrics in a deliberate way as part of a comprehensive approach to writing assessment. Even the staunchest opponents of rubrics have something to learn from the way Ryan endeavors to capitalize on the affordances and mitigate the limitations of this assessment tool.

Ryan is able to wrestle successfully with rubrics because he is, by our definition, an "assessment-literate" educator. What do we mean by this? Our understanding of assessment literacy begins with, but also departs from, that of Rick Stiggins, who has perhaps done more than anyone both to establish the need for teachers' assessment literacy and to provide resources (through his Assessment Training Institute and his books and articles) to help teachers gain it. According to Stiggins,

> Assessment-literate educators . . . come to any assessment knowing what they are assessing, why they are doing so, how best to assess the achievement of interest, how to generate sound examples of performance, what can go wrong, and how to prevent these problems before they occur. (240)

This notion that assessment literacy is rooted in and indexed by what teachers know about assessment is extremely common in what has become a veritable assessment literacy cottage industry. Organizations such as Stiggins's Assessment Training Institute and the SERVE Center at the University of North Carolina at Greensboro and assessment experts such as Stiggins and James Popham have created numerous lists indicating what assessment literate educators know and are able to do.[2] These resources are helpful; we encourage you to read some of the assessment literacy literature on your own. But our goal is not to repeat what these writers and organizations have said, nor to provide yet another laundry list of skills, competencies, and understandings. Rather, we are interested in describing what lies at the core of assessment literacy within the inquiry framework provided by the SARW and our Chapter 1. We believe that approaching assessment literacy within an inquiry framework will help you make good use of the wealth of resources available to you.

From an inquiry perspective, assessment literacy—like literacy itself—is more than a set of knowledge or skills: it is a set of ever-changing social practices rooted in an ongoing process of framing questions, gathering information to answer those questions, analyzing that information, and using that analysis to improve teaching and learning. Thinking of assessment literacy this way makes it both more and less complex than those lists of skills and understandings make it appear. This approach makes assessment literacy more complex because it recognizes assessment literacy as a *form* of literacy, not just a shorthand way of saying "knowing a lot about assessment." Recall from Chapter 1 that NCTE uses the plural form of literacy in "Definition of 21st Century *Literacies*." According to NCTE, literacies "are multiple, dynamic, and malleable." They are also shaped by specific contexts: "they are inextricably linked with particular histories, life possibilities, and social trajectories of individuals and groups." Assessment literacy, as a *form* of literacy, is a complex, uneven, in flux process. That's why we titled the previous section "Ryan Wrestles with Rubrics." What makes Ryan assessment-literate is not only *what* he knows but also *how* he thinks. He is able to inquire into the limitations and affordances of rubrics, using what he knows about writing and assessment to develop a comprehensive approach to teaching and assessing writing.

Assessment Literacy in an Inquiry Framework

- Ask relevant, meaningful questions about teaching and learning.

- Gather information to answer those questions.

- Analyze the information.

- Use the information to improve teaching and learning.

Don't get us wrong: we believe teachers need to know the difference between formative and summative assessment and between selected-response and constructed-response tests. (And so do the framers of the SARW, as evidenced by the inclusion of a glossary of key assessment terms.) But the core thing teachers need to know and be able to do is inquiry itself. We need to know how to *ask relevant, meaningful questions*, the answers to which will help us teach and our students learn. We need to know how to *gather information* about students' writing, using a wide range of methods, including observation, discussion, conferencing, and of course reading and analyzing their writing, including informal writing, reflective pieces, drafts, revisions, portfolios, etc. We need to know how to *analyze the information* we gather, reading it as general readers or as prospective audience members, evaluating it against predetermined criteria, or examining it for trends (in groups, classes, programs, etc.). And we need to know how to *use that information* to improve teaching and learning: by providing feedback to individuals or groups; modeling or promoting self-assessment; generating an evaluation (a score or a grade); making a decision (e.g., whether a student is properly placed, promoted, or allowed to graduate); altering curriculum and instruction to focus on particular writing practices, features, or skills; and so on.

If a lot of this just sounds like good teaching, you're on to something. Writing assessment, as we define it, is embedded within writing instruction; it is an extension of the work we do every day as teachers—and in this sense it's less complex, more elemental, than the literature sometimes makes it out to be. Classroom teachers do not need to develop sophisticated technical knowledge to assess effectively in their classrooms. As James McMillan writes,

> Generally, teachers do not calculate reliability estimates, standard error of measurement, validity coefficients, item discriminations, or standard scores, nor do they construct detailed test blueprints. These techniques are based on principles for developing large-scale objective tests, with limited relevance to the assessment context of the classroom. (34)

Instead, assessment-literate teachers need to approach assessment as "an ongoing activity that involves gathering, interpreting and evaluating information, and action, based on results" (39).

Inquiry always begins with a *lack* of knowledge; it is always a response to curiosity, doubt, wonderment. We turn to it because the complex nature of our work as teachers often requires us to act in the face of considerable uncertainty. Inquiry is a survival skill for those who live with uncertainty. And anyone who takes inquiry seriously understands its self-perpetuating nature: questions, more often than not, lead to further questions. Sometimes the best assessments allow us to ask better—more appropriate, relevant, or nuanced—questions.

For the remainder of the chapter, we turn to four examples of teachers gaining assessment literacy through inquiring into student writing—both texts and practices. These examples hardly exhaust the concept of assessment literacy, but they illustrate some of the ways assessment-literate teachers gather, analyze, and use information about student writing to support student writers in their classrooms. They also show how teachers with varying approaches move assessment to the center of their professional practice—and how they and their students benefit as a result.

In our first example, eighth-grade teacher Anya Bent begins an inquiry project designed to explore classroom uses of formative writing assessments and ends up teaching herself and her students a great deal about what writing is and what writers do.

Anya and Her Students Embark on a Writing Adventure: Using Assessment to Motivate Student Writers

When Anya began her thesis project in the winter of 2009, she had little idea that she would be embarking on what she now calls a "writing adventure" with her students. Her school, on Massachusetts's North Shore, had received a grant to develop performance assessments for English language arts, and she decided to pilot formative performance assessments mainly because she wanted to learn more about them. She decided to incorporate these assessments throughout her Holocaust unit. This unit's "crown jewel," as Anya calls it, has always been a major essay assignment, and her expectation was that she and her students would continue to emphasize this project. But for the purposes of her research, she designed a series of small formative writing assessments that asked students to complete a two-phase drawing activity, regular informal responses to readings, and a poetry writing assignment.

Anya was anxious about these low-stakes writing activities; after all, her students—caught between elementary school and high school, on the verge of but not quite at academic maturity—weren't always the most motivated students. It was hard enough to get many of them to invest in the crown jewel; would they take these less shiny activities seriously?

In fact, Anya empathized. She was struggling with her thesis, especially the section where she needed to provide readers with context about her school and its students. This section just wasn't fun to write. She wanted to get to the narrative sections, where she would tell about her students and their learning—her own crown jewel.

As she began the Holocaust unit, Anya decided to bring her own writing experience into her classroom, expressly positioning herself as a writer alongside her students. She began reading sections of her thesis to her students. "I shared with them the fact that all writing cannot be fun," she says, "but that writing is a way of expressing feeling, disseminating information, and sharing what you know with a reading audience." Her students asked Anya if she enjoyed the writing, and she was honest with them: not always. She enjoyed *having written* but not always the act of writing itself. Still, she knew her writing was helping her to learn about something important to her and to accomplish her personal and professional goals, and so she kept at it. She explained to her students that she and her advisor were "chunking out" the thesis project, which helped her tackle—and even enjoy—the smaller pieces. She explained that this was why she had designed their writing assignments for the Holocaust unit in the same way. Throughout the unit, she shared small sections of her thesis with students, even inviting them to provide feedback for her drafts in progress. This allowed students to see that Anya's writing, like theirs, was not perfect and required time and attention.

Anya began to realize that these smaller chunks of the project, especially when she received helpful feedback on them, were not only helping her move the project forward, but were also energizing her, helping her to enjoy the writing adventure as it unfolded. She wanted to provide her young writers with the same experience through the formative assessments she had designed.

She began with a drawing activity that was, in Anya's words, "simple . . . but extremely telling." She asked students to create a picture of themselves as writers and to include a brief caption. Surprisingly, a majority of students, even those who earned high grades in English, drew pictures that represented frustration and feelings of incompetence about writing (see Figure 2.1).

Figure 2.1. Anya's students draw pictures of themselves as writers.

Emily's initial self-portrait as a writer: "I am too much of an over analist. I read too much into things. I never think it's good enough. (I don't really throw tables.) I also stress out way too much."

Danielle's initial self-portrait as a writer: "When I'm writing, I get fustrated. I'm confused and annoyed that I have to do it, its hard to get ideas."

Francesca's initial self-portrait as a writer: "I'm a timid, unconfident writer. I'm scared to break out of my shell and use all my potential."

"I had not thought, prior to this," Anya says, "that my A students struggled or had low self-images as writers." But the drawing activity taught her "that what [she] thought were simple little writing assignments would be stressful to all the students." These realizations caused Anya to make several changes to her curriculum, including spacing out the assignments and incorporating more group work so students could support one another. However simple, the drawing activity "helped [Anya] to tailor the Holocaust unit to serve the needs of all students."

Anya got to know her students as writers even better through the poem assignment, which came midway through the Holocaust unit. Initially, Anya says, she intended this assignment—which involved writing a poem about the experiences of the main character in a book they were reading—to be a *reading* assessment: she conceived it as a check on reading comprehension. Because she was focused on the content of the poems, Anya provided no further directions on length or style, and she de-emphasized grammar and other mechanics. But as she began reading the poems, Anya knew she had much more than a reading assessment: "[T]he poems were meaningful, deep, and contained the voice of the writers, each unique in the writer's 'spin' on the main character's experience."

The Sadness Is Always There

In a life filled with death and fear
The sadness is always there
A life where the dread of death is near
Upon your shoulder whispering in your ear
In a place where there is nowhere left to hide
I must try to defy a life I see in your eyes
Deep in your soul I try to find a stepping stone
In a world where life is rare
The sadness is always there.

—Ken

Hope

From Poland to Germany,
From bad to worse,
Fright and fear,
And nearly a hearse

Yet these girls were strong,
They beat the odds,
But frightening it was,
Like fish on the rods

Across the snow,
Over the hills,
The terrain was tough,
With many sad kills

The hope was low,
But they did keep on,

The pain and Suffering,
Was what made it wrong.

The food for eating,
Was suited for dogs,
Being skinny and thin,
They were treated like hogs

The world was cruel,
Evil was real,
Insanity was true,
Yet there was a deal

To put to rest,
The death and madness,
For now we hope,
For an end to the sadness

—Tristan

Anya also knew that the poems had to be shared—she should not be the only person to enjoy them—so she asked for volunteers to read their poems aloud to the class. Another surprise: every one of her students volunteered, including the students who had drawn themselves as frustrated and incompetent writers.

Anya was coming to realize that she need not have been anxious about students' response to these smaller writing assignments. While the assignments allowed her to gather, analyze, and use information about students' writing, students were not experiencing them as scary "tests." Indeed, Anya says that for many students, these assessments "were almost more important than the finale," and they led to some of the most interesting and thoughtful classroom discussions of the year.

Why were these smaller assignments so successful? They helped build students' confidence—just as breaking her thesis into chunks was doing for Anya—allowing them multiple ways to engage with the Holocaust material. Also, *because* they were not "about" grades, just as Anya's work on individual sections of her thesis was not about her grade, these assignments emphasized students' learning, and this motivated them. "What we both learned," she says, "was that learning does count, especially if the subject matter means something to the students and the students feel confident in their abilities." In the end, the formative assessments turned out to be "far more impressive measures of their writing than the purported 'jewel' writing assessment." Just as she was able to do her best work when not overwhelmed by the enormity of the writing task, so too were Anya's students as they undertook manageable, meaningful writing activities.

At the inception of Anya's thesis project, she thought of the formative assessments as stepping stones to—a way of gauging students' preparation for—the essay assignment. But her students were helping her to see that formative assessments were "extremely rewarding and informative" in their own right. They allowed her to learn a great deal about her students, both individually and as a group, and to adjust her instruction. It was at this point, Anya says, that she "began to realize that writing assessments were not all about rules, lessons, and rubrics. Writing assessments were more about the writers being comfortable with their own writing."

> **I began to realize that writing assessments were not all about rules, lessons, and rubrics. Writing assessments were more about the writers being comfortable with their own writing.**
>
> **—Anya Bent**

Recognizing the success of these formative assessments, Anya continued to design and implement small, low-stakes writing assignments for students throughout the Holocaust unit. She began to use all of these assignments as opportunities both to gauge students' understanding and engagement with the reading content *and* to learn about and support their writing.

By the time the culminating writing project for the unit rolled around, Anya could see that her students felt much more comfortable as writers. Their task was to take on the persona of a reporter and write an article that connected the youth of today with the youth of the Holocaust period. She was interested in the kinds of connections students would draw between their own lives and the life of Holocaust survivor Sonia Weitz. For Anya's formal assessment of the articles, she used her district's fairly traditional traits-based rubric. Anya explains what happened next:

> The results were twofold. I found the writing to be solid, but the rubric to be weak. What I was grading the students on was not a true reflection of the growth in writing over time (and some of the students who tried really hard were leveled "limited" or "unsatisfactory," and came away with a sense of failure, even if they had progressed in their writing). The students made very good connections between Sonia, themselves, and the world of today. Some understood the connection on a world level, while others understood the connection on a school level. The rubric, however, was not tailored to the writing assignment, so it was misleading.

Anya was particularly impressed that "the teen voice [of the narrators] was loud, clear, concise, and entertaining." She attributes this to the formative assessments and to students' resulting growth in self-confidence. Unfortunately, the rubric did not assess this feature of the writing. "Sometimes," Anya reflects, "the constraints of a rubric can ruin the intent of the teacher, as it did with this assignment."

Still, Anya was pleased by the quality of students' writing and especially their growth, and she adjusted her grading to account for those strengths she found in the writing that were not reflected in the rubric. At the end of the unit, she asked the students to draw themselves as writers again (see Figure 2.2). Anya explains what she learned when she compared the two sets of drawings:

> What I found was dramatic. Those students who were balling up papers, steam rolling out of their ears, throwing pencils, and pounding fists, were now smiling. Even though the rubric in the final writing assignment failed to show their progress as writers, the pictures told me a better story. Students assessed themselves, beginning and end, and proved to themselves through the simple assessment of drawing that they had advanced as writers.

Anya's own writing adventure mirrored those of her students. At the end of her project, she was required by her college to deliver a PowerPoint presentation. She decided to practice the presentation with her students. The response, according to Anya, was "honest, fantastic, and very useful to me." She received many suggestions about the content and her presentation skills. The students even asked her to present again after making the changes they suggested, and she did so—this time with more confidence and poise. Her students showed Anya that they, like her, had learned the power of formative performance assessment.

Figure 2.2. Students draw themselves as writers again after Anya revises her curriculum.

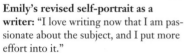

Emily's revised self-portrait as a writer: "I love writing now that I am passionate about the subject, and I put more effort into it."

Danielle's revised self-portrait as a writer: "I feel like I have grown so much as a writer. The words come from deep down and I am proud."

Francesca's revised self-portrait as a writer: "I feel like I've finally stepped outside the box with my writing."

Anya's experience reminds us that writing assessment can be a tool to help motivate students as writers. Assessment-literate teachers, we believe, design innovative assessments that allow students to build self-confidence. But how can we build students' self-confidence while gaining a realistic picture of their current abilities and holding them to high standards? How can we be fair to all students while allowing each student room to flourish? Amy Woods, also an eighth-grade teacher, helps us understand that motivating students to take a step forward from wherever they are is the key to fair and equitable assessment.

Amy Sets Up Students for Success: Using Assessment to Help Students Climb the Writing Ladder

When Amy's students enter her English language arts classroom on Massachusetts's Cape Cod, they are on various rungs of what she calls "the writing ladder." Some students struggle to read and write on grade level, while others are already reading and writing on a tenth-grade level or beyond. But Amy's job, as she sees it, is to help students move up the ladder from whatever rung they occupy when they enter her classroom. Amy understands that the number of rungs students can climb, and the speed with which they can do so, is dependent on a variety of factors, including their effort, cognitive ability, and prior knowledge and experiences, as well as her performance and dedication as a teacher.

Assessment plays a key role in helping students climb the writing ladder. Amy explains: "In a good writing assessment, every child is able to start on a different rung of the ladder without my having to make up different [versions] of the assessment." The assessment should encourage students to reach for the depth and complexity that is within their grasp—the next rung of the ladder.

The key principle Amy keeps in mind as she designs assessments is to set up each student for success, not failure. This principle is the essence of the first standard of the IRA–NCTE *Standards for the Assessment of Reading and Writing:* "The interests of the student are paramount in assessment" (11). As the authors of the SARW suggest, "we must aim for assessment to serve, not harm, each and every student" (11). Amy adds:

> [This principle] sounds simple, but it can be difficult to make happen if you have a rigid mindset and method. I make sure my students have all of the background information before giving the assessment and I make sure they have multiple entry points into the writing assessment. I also need to give students many chances to show mastery.

Amy's fall project shows how she does this. In her school, one of the primary tasks of the eighth-grade ELA curriculum is to teach students to write thesis-driven essays in preparation for academic writing in high school. As the sole ELA eighth-grade teacher, Amy spends the first three months of the school year teaching students how to craft thesis statements, identify and use textual evidence to support their thesis statements, and introduce and conclude their essays. Students write four or five of these essays in rapid succession. In December they take a benchmark essay exam. Students who do not meet a minimum threshold on this exam must revise their essays until they meet that threshold.

Although Amy begins the year providing the same kind of feedback and scaffolding for each student, she tailors her instruction to individual students as the term progresses. For instance, she might give students a choice between two thesis statements at the beginning of the term, but for the second essay, she will challenge each student to write and share an original thesis statement, engaging the class in collaborative brainstorming. Amy explains that she "want[s] them to bounce ideas off of each other and engage in the writing process; this collaborative process allows all the different levels of writers in my class to develop a thesis that they will be able to prove." As the school year progresses, students share their thesis statements less and less, though Amy continues to check them. When students are stuck, Amy asks questions: "Do you think this character made the right choice?" "Do you think this character regrets his decision?" "What is the conflict in this story?" Amy says that "by asking these questions, I lead students on a path toward creating their own thesis statement and this helps them much more than if I just gave them a list to choose from. Now they are invested in their essay because they came up with an idea that means something to them."

An important part of being assessment-literate is knowing how to undertake assessment in ways that are, as Standard 6 of the SARW indicates, "fair and equitable" (20). Amy recognizes that fairness does not mean treating all students the same way. Some students will need more help than others to be successful, and her job is to do what she can to provide the conditions in which they are successful. "I don't write the essay for them," she says. "It's their work. But I do give them the tools they will need. It's up to them to use the tools [effectively]." Her goal is to put more and more of the responsibility for the writing process in students' hands, and that will happen at a different pace for different students. With *all* students, she takes a step back as the school year continues. However, Amy is quick to add, aside from the state test and the benchmark essay test, "I will always check Johnny's brainstorm paper because he needs to do one or else his essay goes off topic. I will always sit and spellcheck with Samantha because she is a poor speller and I don't want that to get in the way of her great ideas. I will always sit next to Zack and ask him questions about what he is writing because he is too brief." Again, her goal is to set up each student for success.

> **The key to meeting each learner at his or her level is to *know* each student.**
> **—Amy Woods**

What does "success" mean to Amy? Of course, one of her goals is to prepare students to pass the benchmark exam. But her chief aim is to help students, no matter their present level of ability or experience with academic writing, to "combine their creative, analytical, and practical knowledge to write an interesting, in-depth, clear piece of writing." To this end, she uses constant feedback and scaffolding:

> I work really hard each fall to give students appropriate and timely feedback. This feedback comes in all forms. It can be written—on rough copies, partial rough copies, full rough copies. It can be oral: sitting with each child to hammer out his thesis, sitting down next to a student as he types. It may be question-based: *What are you proving in this paragraph? What does this mean? Can you find a quote to back this up? Where is your topic sentence?* It may be directive: *You need to make this clearer. Let's find a quote that helps to prove this. You need to capitalize the main character's name.* It depends on what the child needs. Students who are at a higher level in writing ability can take one of my questions and run with it. Students who have a hard time organizing one paragraph, let alone four or five, need more directive feedback to feel successful. Most of my feedback is a combination of the two.

As Amy suggests, "The key to meeting each learner at his or her level is to *know* each student." Standard 4 of the SARW insists that "[a]ssessment must reflect and allow for critical inquiry into curriculum and instruction" (16); while Amy certainly uses assessment this way, she also uses it as a means for conducting critical inquiry into students themselves. She is able to make quick but effective judgments about what students need because she is continuously learning about students through her ongoing assessment of their writing:

> By the second or third essay, I know which students do not need to fill out a brain-storm paper completely, which students need me to help them write topic sentences so they don't go off course, which ones need extra time, and which ones need help spellchecking. I know who doesn't put in punctuation and who doesn't seem to know where the shift key is to make a capital letter. I know who will rush a conclusion and who will not open a book to find a quote unless I am sitting down next to him.

When responding to student writing, Amy feels it is imperative to demonstrate her own commitment to students' learning. "If the assessment is meaningful to me," she says, "then it is meaningful to them."

Make no mistake: Amy's approach to teaching and assessing writing requires time, effort, and flexibility:

> There are classes where I am jumping from one essay to the next. In the span of ten minutes, I might be working on four different essays. One child might be on his second page and have the most creative analysis I've seen, while the next is struggling with his intro paragraph or can't find a quote to back up an idea because he has trouble with comprehension.

But for Amy, this hands-on, intensive approach, which embeds assessment throughout the curriculum, is worth it both because it helps her deepen her understanding of her students as they progress and because she is able to watch her students, many of whom enter her classroom in September hating to write, "buy in" to the process and improve their confidence and their abilities, thus allowing them to climb the writing ladder.

Though Anya and Amy approach the teaching and assessing of writing differently in their classrooms, they both demonstrate how assessment-literate teachers use writing assessment to inquire into their students' writing so that they can engage those writers and encourage them to improve. Our next example, from the classroom of Missouri high school teacher Melissa Lynn Pomerantz, emphasizes how she involves students in self-assessment through the use of digital writing forums such as blogs.

Melissa Goes Digital: Using Writing Assessment to Sponsor Student Reflection

Rather than teach a traditional research paper, in years when her teaching schedule permits Melissa asks her sophomores to collaborate in small groups to create a documentary film. Melissa undertakes this work because she believes "the nature of writing is changing in the world and in order for our students to be successful in life after high school, they must be able to compose in digital mediums as well as traditional pen and paper genres." Through the documentary film project, not only do Melissa's students research, storyboard, write, film, and edit a five-minute segment that is combined into a whole-class documentary film, but they also maintain blogs on which they document, reflect, and assess their work on the film. As technology shifts the way we teach writing in this brave new world, Melissa has found that new technologies such as blogs can serve as a space for students to self-assess and reflect on their writing.

Initially, Melissa incorporated blogging as part of the documentary project work for a very practical purpose: "I wanted the students to have a single place for all of their writing and thinking. The research, planning, writing, and assessing are all on their blogs to help them stay organized." Melissa's students maintained their blogs for about two months and used them as sites for various tasks, including summarizing research, brainstorming ideas, and communicating with other members of the class. However, over the course of experimenting with blogs, Melissa observed something else: students were becoming quite adept at assessing their own writing.

> **As students learn to compose in a new media, it is important to provide a space for them to assess and reflect on their learning process.**
> —**Melissa Lynn Pomerantz**

Assessment-literate teachers help their students assess their own work. This does not necessarily mean having students grade themselves; indeed, some research suggests that the introduction of self-grading into more general self-assessment and self-reflection has neutral or even deleterious effects on learning (Andrade). Rather, we are thinking of assessments in which students become an important source of information about their own learning and writing—the kinds of assessments called for in the very first standard of the SARW ("The interests of the student are paramount in assessment"): those that "encourage students to become engaged in literacy learning, to reflect on their own reading and writing in productive ways, and to set respective literacy goals" (11). This is precisely what we see Melissa's students doing on their reflective blogs as they develop their documentary films.

Marty, for instance, provides insight into his group's progress in the way only a teen can explain it. Notice how Marty is able to keep track of where he and his group members are in their process while also setting goals for future work.

> Yesterday was a day of some solid progress on my group's segment of the documentary. Greg, Kelsey, and I were coming up with ideas like crazy. We were active all class and had no brain farts so I'm feeling pretty confident on the things we've come up with so far. We also have some good footage thanks to our hard work. Let's see... we have video of my car's exhaust and some other car footage we edited multiple times, but we haven't recorded some other footage that we think would be totally radical visual metaphors. Also, I worked on creating my storyboard. I did some hardcore thinking about appealing camera angles for different parts of our segment and I came up with excellent ideas. More brainstorming with my crew might make it too good. And finally, our interviews. We haven't received confirmation from any "experts" to come and do an interview which is a bummer, but there are some experts at school we could fall back on if it's necessary. Street interviews are tomorrow and I think we're going to kill it. From what I've heard from our practice interviews, my group has mad interviewing skills.

In this post, Marty begins by praising the work of his group and their recent footage and editing, but he notes the need for additional filming. He then discusses his individual tasks of storyboarding and creating appropriate camera angles before addressing the difficulty in pinning down an "expert" to interview and the work the group plans to accomplish tomorrow in class. In other blog posts, Marty discussed the quality of their video footage, the need to edit their footage to meet their purpose, recording the audio for voice-overs, and how much if any help he and his group members needed from their teacher. The blogs both gave students practice writing with new media and allowed them to self-assess. "As students learn to compose in a new media," Melissa says, "it is important to provide a space for them to assess and reflect on their learning process. In a large project like creating a documentary film, the blog serves as a space for students to take a moment and assess how well their group is working, the needs of the group, and the work they need to accomplish."

In addition to reflecting on their group process, Melissa's students used their blogs to reflect on issues of audience and content. For instance, students spent a lot of time blogging about creating an appropriate title and introduction for their film. In the following post, Edward connects the tone of the title with his intended audience and the ability of the title to capture the larger purpose of the documentary:

> We may not want to get too creative on the title of this documentary. For example, something that just simply rhymes or a funny but not effective slogan. If people watching get a feeling that this is not a very serious documentary, they may not take any of it seriously which would make the documentary pointless. We could probably make the title Global Warming, with a convincing picture in the background to add to the overall effect. The introduction could be the first section of our documentary.

While Edward doesn't provide any of the titles he and his group were considering, his awareness of the importance of the title to the goals his group was attempting to accomplish comes through in his blog post. Further, this entry shows Edward assessing his writing alongside some of the larger rhetorical concepts Melissa was introducing to her students in the unit, including awareness of audience and purpose.

Kelsey, too, reflects on her difficulty in coming up with a title and opening image for her group's portion of the documentary.

> I'm definitely having trouble coming up with a title. "The Truth About Global Warming" is the best I can come up with, but that really isn't catchy or original at all. I'll keep thinking about it and write a new post if I come up with something exciting.
>
> I think that the introduction should be really catchy. I'm not sure how many people are going to like this idea, but I was thinking about starting with a scene from the 1950s with a kid saying something like, "Gee, Ma! It's so hot outside I could fry an egg on the sidewalk!" Then we could completely change the tone of the video with serious music and go into how someday that could be possible because the earth is getting so warm. Then we could flash shocking statistics and catch the audience's attention for a second time to get them really interested in the topic.

Kelsey's post was more than a moment of self-reflection on her writing process; it also sparked comments from the blog readers. One of Melissa's goals in having her students blog rather than journal about their filmmaking adventures was to provide them the opportunity to write in a public and dynamic forum where conversations can occur. To aid in these conversations, Melissa responded to each of her students' posts and also recruited some help from other high school teachers and members of the community. As Melissa says, "Blogs allow students to get feedback from a wider audience than just me. They get feedback from me, from other students and from outside readers." The day after Kelsey posted about her title and introduction ideas, she received conflicting feedback from Melissa and Kathy Blackmore, a district curriculum coordinator, on how she might start the film.

(Some context on Kathy's post: this was in response to one of Kelsey's earlier posts, in which she explained that her group was considering writing the causes of global warming on an old map a history teacher was going to give them and then setting the map on fire.)

1. Melissa Lynn Pomerantz on May 1, 2008 5:41 am
   We could definitely do a grainy 50's spoof—who should we get to dress up with slicked side-parted hair (boy) or a poodle-skirt (girl)? ☺
   Great idea.
   Keep thinking about titles.
2. Kathy Blackmore on May 1, 2008 7:26 pm
   I love the map idea . . . causes and then the map burning. I am glad you got permission to do it in the parking lot! I think the "hot enough to fry an egg" is a good visual but the title may not pull people in. . . . BUT, I am struggling with any suggestions for titles?? Is there a title like . . . Global Warming: 21st Century on Fire? I will keep thinking. . . . Title is really important to grab the attention…maybe once you put the video together the title will be obvious??

In this exchange, Kelsey states her difficulty coming up with a title and opening image for her group's portion of the film. Melissa affirms the possibility of the 1950s-era opening, but Kathy seems more excited about opening the film with a burning map, even offering a title to incorporate the idea of fire and burning. On her blog, Kelsey is faced with two different audience members providing two different viewpoints on how she and her group members might start their segment of the film. Moments like these are what Melissa had hoped for: "I want students to see the choices they have as they write. Using blogs, students can see themselves thinking out their ideas over time as well as receive input from their readers and then they can decide how to move forward with their project." The blogs, then, help Melissa conduct ongoing assessment of student learning that "involve[s] multiple perspectives" (Standard 8; 24) and is "based in the local school learning community" (Standard 9; 26).

When the film was finally complete, Melissa's students provided a public screening of their film for teachers, students, and community members who helped with interviews or as blog partners. As part of the final assessment of their unit, Melissa asked each of her students to watch the film and write a final blog post in response to the following questions:

1. How well does this documentary fulfill its intended purposes?
   a. To inform
   b. To persuade
   c. To effect change

2. What works in this film?

3. What could work better in this film?

4. What did you learn during this project? Think about what you learned in terms of film, research, topic, blogging, organizing, working with others, writing, anything else you learned.

5. How do you think you will use what you have learned in the future?

As they reflected on these questions, Melissa pointed her students back to a criteria sheet they had created earlier in the unit based on their observations of several short documentaries. For their final assessment, Melissa and her students homed in on the following criteria: content, organization, visual/audio elements, technical aspects, and fluidity and consistency. Below are two brief excerpts from Julia's three-page assessment of her class's documentary.

> . . . Overall, I think that each group did their job on informing our viewers about the topics they had. I think that the persuading part could be worked on a little bit more. I feel as though we were giving more facts than actually persuading. We could have used those facts and change them to be more persuading. I thought that the facts being used were effecting change rather than persuading. Daniel's group did a great job at effecting change. Their visual metaphor of the earth exploding was a great visual that can allow people to see why it is important to change. I think that overall, we did the best at informing people of the information. . . .
>
> . . . I learned that blogging can be fun and that it is fun to know people are reading my work. I learned about organizing a film to having it tell a story and that organizing helps the film make sense. I learned that the order of things are very important and can change what type of message you get from the film. . . .

In her introduction, Julia is quick to move from celebrating the film to articulating her assessment that as a class they did well on informing their audience, but the presentation of information did not rise to the level of persuading the audience. In this section of her self-assessment, Julia assesses the film against the original goals of the project—to inform, persuade, and effect change. Later in her assessment, Julia reflects on the importance of organizing the film in a way that fulfills the message or purpose she and her group members set out to accomplish. Reading the blog post, Melissa can see in Julia's final assessment her ability to examine a documentary film for a filmmaker's intended purpose.

Across Melissa's students' blogs are examples of students inquiring into their process of constructing the film, wrestling with content, choosing images, and revising their writing, as well as assessing their final products. Melissa uses blogging to invite students into the assessment process, from setting goals to tracking their progress to evaluating their final products. Blogs seem an especially appropriate venue because they are for many students a familiar reflective and conversational medium.

At the same time, it cannot be said that self-assessment itself, especially in an academic context, is familiar or comfortable for many students—at least at first. As Melissa's carefully crafted questions for reflection suggest, assessment-literate teachers provide students guidance for self-reflection and self-assessment. For instance, we can work with students to develop *language* to describe what writing is and does. Sometimes, as we saw with Ryan, rubrics provide language that we unpack with students; other times, the language emerges from shared exploration of student writing, as it does in the classroom of Missouri high school teacher Lisa Giljum-Jánský.

Lisa Starts with Student Writing: Using Assessment to Inquire into Writing with Students

Lisa grounds her work as a writing teacher in Nancie Atwell's principles of providing time for students to write, encouraging them to claim ownership over their writing, and responding to their writing in ways that allow them to do further inquiry and revision. She takes seriously Atwell's conviction that "[y]oung writers want to be listened to. . . . They need teachers who will guide them to the meanings they don't know yet by showing them how to build on what they *do* know and *can* do. . . . And they need to be able to anticipate and predict how their teacher will approach them" (218, emphasis in original). However, Lisa teaches 120 students (sometimes more), so individual conferences are not always possible. This is why she developed a "debriefing" process as part of her writing assessment practices. Through this classroom practice, Lisa emphasizes students' strengths, helps them anticipate and predict how readers (including their teacher) will respond to their writing, and provides them with a shared language to describe and assess writing, including their own. Starting always with student writing itself, Lisa guides her young writers as they inquire together into writing—learning how to read, we might say, *as* writers.

To prepare for the debriefing, as Lisa reads a class set of drafts she creates for herself a running list of surprises, issues, and concerns. She explains, "If I notice multiple students are lacking specificity and detail, I not only address the issue through written comments on the students' papers, but I also make a note of the issue on my list. Any reoccurring issue—from structure, to content, to grammar—is included on my list." After providing individual comments, Lisa prioritizes her list, identifying what will become a class handout with "Samples to Celebrate" (Figure 2.3) and "Dos and Don'ts" (Figure 2.4). She then selects excerpts from students' papers to illustrate quality writing to celebrate with the whole class.

Figure 2.3. Lisa's handout, based on her observations about students' writing, identifies samples of student writing to celebrate.

Samples to Celebrate

What is strong about each of the following pieces?
Why have they been selected for the debrief?

Fortunately, with a new semester and a new town, I can almost start over with my life. The memory and embarrassment of setting Mrs. Johnson's lawn on fire while playing with bottle rockets can be forgotten, as well as the "F" I received in chemistry last semester.
This piece has been selected because . . .

Semesters are long monotone, repetitive phases of life, where the average pimple-faced, lethargic teenage human must sit in awkwardly fitted chairs and listen to teachers and grown-ups constantly telling him or her what to do.
This piece has been selected because . . .

A new semester is kind of like a sweater, a brand-new-you-just-bought-it-yesterday-but-can't-wait-to-wear-it-because-if-you-don't-you'll-fall-off-a-cliff-and-die kind of sweater......It itches so much red blotches begin to form on your cellulite infested jiggly arms, and even your teachers start to stare at your weird behavior.
This piece has been selected because . . .

First, you're stunned. Unsure what to think. Then, when you realize that after just two days you already have three papers due, seventy pages to read, and who knows how many math problems, the stress finally begins to kick in. . . . Like that child whose cheeks were burned red from the bitter cold, causing them to seek their mother's comfort, many high-schoolers just want to drop their textbooks, fling their backpacks in a trashcan, and dart out the doors of Hell to lose themselves in the secure embrace of their mother.
This piece has been selected because . . .

Figure 2.4. Lisa provides a mini-lesson on the elements of strong writing.

One-Page Paper Debrief—A new semester is like . . .

Dos

DO use SPECIFIC, PERSONAL, and VIVID examples from your own life.

This essay is about YOU and YOUR LIFE. Talk about specific things that happen in your life. The more specific and detailed your example, the better!

Read the examples, fill in the blanks, and find the PIZZAZZ in these details. Underline, circle, or highlight the pizzazz.

Example:

General specific: One thing I like about a new semester is new classes.

Specific and personal: This semester I am taking painting instead of design crafts. I love it because . . .

Specific, personal, and vivid: This semester I moved from the "try not to papier-mâché your neighbor" world of design crafts to the "I am an ar-tēēst" world of painting.

Weak Example:

General specific: A new semester is a wide open meadow with lots of places to explore and get lost.

Specific and personal:

Specific, personal, and vivid:

As part of her sophomore honors English class, Lisa assigns weekly one-page papers that allow her to work with students on writing concisely, precisely, and in detail on a variety of topics. For the first paper, Lisa asks students to use figurative language while writing about starting a new semester. The papers are due on Mondays and Lisa passes them back with comments on the following Monday. She waits a day after handing back the papers to begin the debriefing process with her students. And on Wednesday, "when they are ready to hear the response and look at their own writing," Lisa asks her students to spend time noticing patterns in the samples to celebrate.

During a recent reading of students' papers, Lisa noticed that students needed additional focus on incorporating specific details. When students came into class, she gave them a handout. On the front side of the handout were samples of student writing to celebrate; on the back, Lisa provided examples for the lessons she wanted to reinforce. Class began this way:

> **Lisa:** Look at the "Samples to Celebrate." Why are they on the "Celebrate" list? What is the writer doing well? Take a minute, turn to a partner, and discuss this.
>
> **Student 1:** I like it. It makes me laugh. I mean, it sounds just like Jordan. Really, only she would write or say something like that.
>
> **Student 2:** Yeah, that's definitely her voice. And I'm betting Giljum wants us to notice the details in here. How specific and personal they are.
>
> **Lisa:** All right, come back to me folks. [as she moves into whole-class discussion] So what do you see? Why is this a strong sample of writing?
>
> **Student 1:** It has voice.
>
> **Lisa:** Okay, keep going. How so? Where?
>
> **Student 1:** I mean, you can tell it's Jordan's. That's her sense of humor. Who else would talk about setting their neighbor's lawn on fire?
>
> **Lisa:** Okay, so her idea has personality, but what other strengths are in that very same line?
>
> **Student 2:** It's specific.
>
> **Lisa:** Is it one of those general specifics we've talked about?
>
> **Student 2:** Nope, specific and personal. And vivid. It's a Jordan detail for sure.
>
> **Student 3:** The bottle rockets, the fire, the F in chemistry are all fun to read. I can relate, I laugh. They make you want to read her essay.
>
> **Lisa:** Okay, so back to your debrief notes for revision. . . . What does this sample show us about detail?

After reviewing each example, students wrote notes on their debrief handouts, identifying what they noticed in the samples and what made the writing worth celebrating. Lisa then moved the students on to the next example. Again, she asked students what they noticed and what made it strong. After working through the examples, Lisa presented a mini-lesson on the "Dos" section (Figure 2.4), providing additional examples to reinforce the students' excerpts and asking students to improve a weak sample. Finally, she asked students to record their observations on a log sheet (Figure 2.5), summarizing student and teacher comments from the debrief and identifying two areas of improvement for their own writing. These logs became running records of students' goals for their writing and their emerging strengths as writers.

Like Melissa's students, Lisa's students are learning to self-reflect and self-assess, setting their own goals and gauging their progress. Both teachers understand, in the words of the SAWR, that "assessment must encourage students to become engaged in literacy learning, to reflect on their own reading and writing in productive ways, and to set respective literacy goals" (11). For Lisa, the key is to involve students in close observation and analysis of their own and one another's writing. She explains, "I am guiding the process, but it is an interactive inquiry into [their writing]." After they analyzed other students' writing, writers turned to their

---

Figure 2.5. Students record their observations on a log sheet to help them improve their writing.

On my revision/next essay:

Dos . . .

Don'ts . . .

Additional Notes:

Individual Writing Goal:

drafts and articulated what they noticed: Did I use vivid, personal details? Did I write in first or second person? How does my conclusion work with the rest of my piece? As Lisa says, "Rather than circle only what is 'wrong,' I ask them what they *can* do and what they need to improve on as a writer."

> **Rather than circle only what is "wrong," I ask them what they *can* do and what they need to improve on as a writer.**
>
> **—Lisa Giljum-Jánský**

The following week, students revised their first drafts, using the debriefing conversation and their log sheet as guides. Lisa noted that students revised more readily with these supports:

> It's important for students to inquire into their own writing. When I use student samples, they comment on and examine other students' writing as well as their own. They describe what they see in the samples and in their first draft. . . . They learn students are good writers and they can begin seeing themselves as writers. They also see that good writers don't always get it right the first time; you write, revise, work with others, and revise some more.

In short, writing is what Lisa's students do *and* what they study. Lisa honors student writing by making it the object of the class's attention. And she honors students by involving them as knowledgeable and insightful readers and assessors of their own writing.

From Assessment Literacy to Assessment Expertise

Certainly it would be possible to show how the teachers we've featured in this chapter meet traditional criteria of "assessment literacy": they use a variety of assessment methods to gather evidence of student learning; they provide appropriate scaffolding to students; they make appropriate instructional modifications; they involve students in self-assessment, etc. More important to us, however, is that each views writing assessment as an integral part of the teaching of writing and as an opportunity—for them and their students—to inquire into writing. Ryan uses writing assessment to sponsor rich conversations with students about writing. Anya uses it to encourage students to experience themselves *as* writers. Amy uses it to help students improve from wherever they are as writers. Melissa uses it to help students reflect on and assess their own writing. Lisa uses it to engage students in focused conversation about writing. These teachers understand that writing-assessment-as-inquiry provides an opportunity to identify, articulate, and support our—and our students'—most cherished values and goals, as discussed in Chapter 1.

These examples also show how teachers with widely varying curricular and instructional emphases—from eating diaries to Holocaust narratives, from thesis-driven essays to blogging—can all, in their own way, move writing assessment to the center of their professional practice. For these teachers, writing assessment is not something that happens at the end of a unit, quarter, or academic year; it is something they are doing all the time as part of their teaching practice. Moreover, they are also involving their students in ongoing assessment-as-inquiry, tapping their considerable knowledge about writing and about themselves as writers. So assessment-as-inquiry is a core activity of learning, too, both for teachers and for students.

Indeed, assessment literacy within an inquiry framework positions teachers and students as both knowers and learners. It recognizes that teachers and students are themselves the most sensitive and important assessment instruments. When they engage in ongoing assessment-as-inquiry, they don't ever need to wait around for the results of tests designed by testing companies or state officials; through careful, attentive, shared inquiry, they know and are coming to know—about their subjects, about one another, about assessment itself—with an intimacy that external assessments could never provide.

In this way, assessment-as-inquiry is a political act. It insists that what teachers and students know—and how they come to know it—matters and should count. This is a thread we pick up in the next chapter, which is devoted to the notion of assessment expertise. Assessment expertise extends beyond classrooms, into and beyond schools. As we show, this work deepens our assessment literacy and broadens its impact, allowing us to acquire the kind of expertise necessary to combat the privatization of teaching that we discussed in the first chapter and to build on the important assessment-as-inquiry foundation that we discuss in this chapter.

Notes

1. The examples featured throughout this book are drawn from the work of actual teachers and students, and the names are real. Because we want to honor teachers' own understandings and insights, we draw liberally on written descriptions and explanations they provided to us, and we include classroom artifacts whenever possible. Our own descriptions and explanations are drawn from conversations with and observations of the teachers. In each instance, teachers had the final say in what was included in the examples and how they were presented. We are immensely grateful to the teachers and students who gave permission for their work to be showcased in this book and who collaborated so generously with us to shape the representations of that work.

2. For example, Stiggins's list includes
    1. Starting with clear purposes
    2. Focusing on achievement targets
    3. Selecting proper assessment methods
    4. Sampling student achievement
    5. Avoiding bias or distortion (240–42)

The SERVE Center at the University of North Carolina at Greensboro claims that assessment literate teachers know:

1. How to define clear learning goals.
2. How to make use of a variety of assessment methods to gather evidence of student learning.
3. How to analyze achievement data (both quantitative and qualitative) and make good inferences from the data gathered.
4. How to provide appropriate feedback to students.
5. How to make appropriate instructional modifications.
6. How to involve students in self-assessment.
7. How to engineer a classroom assessment environment that boosts student motivation to learn.

James Popham, in "Assessment Literacy Project" for the Kansas Department of Education, provides a series of short videos on a range of assessment topics, including (among others) formative and summative assessment; alignment with standards; fairness; learning progressions; test validity and reliability; selected-response, constructed-response, and performance assessments; assessing students with disabilities and English language learners; and large-scale assessment.

Developing Writing Assessment Expertise

We want to argue loudly and clearly that practitioners who are deeply engaged in the work of teaching and learning know something about that work and, collectively with one another and with others, including parents and community groups, have the capacity to generate and critique knowledge, figure out how to use (or not use) knowledge generated by others, improve practice, and enhance students' life chances.

—Marilyn Cochran-Smith and
Susan L. Lytle, *Inquiry as Stance* (125)

The remedy is not to have one expert dictating educational methods and subject-matter to a body of passive, recipient teachers, but the adoption of intellectual initiative, discussion, and decisions throughout the entire school corps.

—John Dewey, "Democracy in Education" (196)

I t seems more than a little ironic that Marilyn Cochran-Smith and Susan Lytle, authors of the influential 1993 book *Inside/Outside: Teacher Research and Knowledge*, find themselves sixteen years later having "to argue loudly and clearly" that engaged teachers "know something about [their] work" (*Inquiry* 6). Their earlier book, after all, helped spawn a teacher research movement. (See the sidebar for books on teacher inquiry.)

Books on Teacher Inquiry

Composing a Teacher Study Group: Learning about Inquiry in Primary Classrooms, Richard J. Meyer, Linda Brown, Elizabeth DeNino, Kimberly Larson, Mona McKenzie, Kimberly Ridder, and Kimberly Zetterman

Inquiry as Stance: Practitioner Research for the Next Generation, Marilyn Cochran-Smith and Susan L. Lytle

On Teacher Inquiry: Approaches to Language and Literacy Research, Dixie Goswami, Ceci Lewis, Marty Rutherford, and Diane Waff

Reclaiming the Classroom: Teacher Research as an Agency for Change, Dixie Goswami and Peter R. Stillman, eds.

Teacher Research for Better Schools, Marian M. Mohr, Courtney Rogers, Betsy Sanford, Mary Ann Nocerino, Marion S. MacLean, and Sheila Clawson

Teaching as Inquiry: Asking Hard Questions to Improve Practice and Student Achievement, Alexandra Weinbaum, David Allen, Tina Blythe, Katherine Simon, Steve Seidel, and Catherine Rubin

Teaching as the Learning Profession: Handbook of Policy and Practice, Linda Darling-Hammond and Gary Sykes

But as the authors note, even as teacher inquiry has blossomed over the past two decades, many countervailing forces have been working against its full realization. The standards and accountability movement, top-down models of educational reform, standardized testing, the rhetoric of "best practices," NCLB-inspired "scientism," and an ever-tighter yoking of education to the economy have de-emphasized "local contexts, local knowledge, and the role of teachers as decision-makers and change agents" (6). These developments take education out of the hands of teachers, minimizing or ignoring their expertise. This is especially the case with assessment, which, as we have noted, is often treated as something done *to* or *for* teachers and students, not something teachers and their students do.

This chapter encourages teachers to develop and share writing assessment expertise. This, we know, will sound like a daunting proposition; again and again we hear teachers say, "I'm no assessment expert; I'm just a teacher." But as we hope to have shown in Chapter 2, assessment is part of teaching and learning, not an abstract technical science, and it falls well within the professional purview of teachers. And as we hope to demonstrate in this chapter, writing assessment expertise *is* achievable by teachers, especially when they work together, as Cochran-Smith and Lytle propose.

Inquiry and Expertise

Let's begin with the notion of expertise itself. Typically, we think of experts as having specialized, often technical, knowledge or skills. Their authority derives from their possession of a body of knowledge or a set of skills that others, so-called lay people, don't have. We defer to the judgment of experts—the doctors who diagnose our ailments or the lawyers who steer us through complex legal issues— because we recognize (or assume) that their judgment is informed by training and experience.

Training and experience are also necessary for teachers, of course. To be effective, we must not only master our subjects but also understand how students learn those subjects and the most effective ways to teach them. To do this, teachers must understand how diverse students learn and develop; how to use assessment strategies to diagnose, monitor, and motivate student learning; how to choose or design appropriate teaching methods and strategies; how to create disciplined, engaging learning environments; how to develop curriculum within larger scopes and sequences; how to collaborate with one another and with other educational partners to promote learning; how to critically examine our practice in order to improve it . . . and more.

Unfortunately, teachers' professional judgment is not often viewed with the same respect as is a doctor's or a lawyer's. Instead of investing in the development of teachers' professional judgment, many educational reforms over the past couple decades have been aimed at restricting, circumventing, or even replacing that judgment. For example, the No Child Left Behind Act defines *scientifically based* teaching in ways that render invisible most forms of teacher research in favor of controlled experimental or quasi-experimental studies (see Gallagher, *Reclaiming*; Liston, Whitcomb, and Borko). Moreover, the "best practices" mindset supported by the law and the US Department of Education's What Works Clearinghouse suggests that we will be able to identify a stable body of "method and techniques" that will be equally effective wherever and with whomever they are tried, thereby discouraging ongoing innovation and inviting what John Dewey called a "rigid orthodoxy" and "a dead monotonous uniformity of practice" ("Progressive" 172). This mindset, relying as it does on a "technicist" understanding of expertise, reduces teaching to transportable methods and techniques, leaving out the important adaptive work that is at the center of teacher practice.

After all, teachers—like doctors or lawyers—are not technicians, people who deploy their practical knowledge to solve technical problems. We are constantly faced with complex, novel problems, and we must inquire into their complexity, drawing on our training and experience, to render sound professional judgment. Our expertise, then, consists not only of knowledge and skill but also of what Donald Schön calls "reflection-in-action," or the kind of continuous inquiry that is required to meet uncertainty (27). (This is also true of other professions; see, for instance, both Cassell and Gawande on the medical profession.) This type of expertise is dynamic and can be gained only in what Cochran-Smith and Lytle call the "dialectic of inquiry and practice" (*Inquiry* 93).

Assessment Expertise in an Inquiry Framework

- Practice reflection-in-action.

- Engage in dialectic of inquiry and practice.

- Collaborate with colleagues to pool expertise.

- Collaborate with noneducators to borrow, extend, and share expertise.

A dialectic suggests movement: a constant back-and-forth, putting two things—here inquiry and practice—into conversation with each other. If this is how teachers' expertise is produced, then it follows that neither expertise nor the process that generates it can be codified once and for all. For Cochran-Smith and Lytle, inquiry is best thought of not as a method, strategy, or formula, but as a *stance*. By this, they mean a way of knowing, a habit of mind, even a worldview (*Inquiry* viii). Understood this way, inquiry is not confined to a particular project or time period; it is embedded in teachers' professional practice in all sites of their work (121).

Inquiry is a core concept in the IRA–NCTE *Standards for the Assessment of Reading and Writing* (SARW). As we discussed in Chapter 2, the authors implore teachers to move away from a transmission-based approach to teaching and learning and to adopt instead an inquiry model. In addition, Standard 4 reads, "Assessment must reflect and allow for critical inquiry into curriculum and instruction" (16). We showed in Chapter 2 how teachers are using assessment to inquire into writing itself as well as into their students as writers. For these teachers—indeed, for the teachers discussed throughout this book—moving assessment to the center of their professional practice means committing to inquiry as an ongoing practice, which is why Cochran-Smith and Lytle's notion of an inquiry *stance* as a way of knowing and doing is so critical to developing writing assessment expertise.

The inquiry stance can take different forms, but it always involves building expertise by moving back and forth between inquiry and practice. This kind of expertise, gained through the lived experience of teaching and learning with students as well as careful inquiry into that experience, is available only to those who spend their days doing this work. This is *professional* expertise, and it matters, or should matter, for the same reason professional expertise matters in other professions: not because it is infallible (no professional knowledge attains that status), but because it is situated, grounded within ongoing inquiry and practice.

The examples in this chapter illustrate various approaches to the inquiry–practice dialectic. Once again, the specific projects and school contexts differ, but at the heart of each example is a teacher working in collaboration with others—students, colleagues, community members, and parents—to gain expertise in writing assessment. Notice that these collaborators are also situated to provide particular kinds of expertise, and sometimes that expertise can have a multiplier effect on teachers' own expertise. It is important to remember that expertise is not a zero-sum game. Standard 2 of the SARW proposes that "[t]he teacher is the most important agent of assessment" (13), but not the only one. Indeed, other standards call for assessment processes that involve "multiple perspectives" (Standard 8; 24) and "active and essential participation of families and community members" (Standard 9; 26). But because the teachers are working day-in and day-out with students, they have privileged access to knowledge and strategies involving teaching and learning.

In our first example, Angie Muse and her colleagues work within a familiar model—a district-assigned "data team"—to enact the inquiry–practice dialectic that Cochran-Smith and Lytle advocate.

Angie's Data Team at Work: The Dialectic of Inquiry and Practice

Generally speaking, data teams provide a structure in which teachers convene to examine student work, usually in the form of assessment results, and collaboratively plan curriculum and instruction. Some data teams survey a wide range of data sources, whereas others focus exclusively on common formative assessment data. Some are administratively driven, while others are inquiry based and teacher driven. In any event, the two core activities of data teams are analysis of learning results and collaborative planning.

> **Assessment is an ongoing process that is woven together with focused and purposeful instruction.**
>
> —Angie Muse

Angie's district requires that teachers meet monthly in data teams, but teachers in her building, including Angie and her fellow eighth-grade teachers, decided to meet twice a month to make more time to share their observations. According to Angie, the core activity of her data team is inquiry. Her team is tasked with ensuring that district goals are met, but for Angie and her colleagues, their meetings are also opportunities to share with and learn from one another and to plan together. For example, in a recent discussion of students' written summaries (a district requirement for all eighth graders), Angie and her colleagues found themselves returning to the district rubric. Here is Angie's reconstruction of the conversation:

Diane: It says a 4-point or advanced summary will have an "effective beginning, middle, and end." The 3-point or proficient summary has a "clear beginning, middle, and end."

Angie: What exactly is an effective beginning for a summary?

Robert: Well, they have to have a main idea there.

Jana: When I think effective beginnings, I think of an attention-getting lead.

Angie: For a summary, too?

> **Diane:** Do we really expect writers to capture a reader's attention in a summary? I've never had my students do that in a summary.
>
> **Robert:** Well, what *do* we expect?
>
> **Angie:** We need to think about summaries in the real world. When do people do summaries of informational texts? Why do they do it? When the summary is done for another person, what does that reader need?

Here we see this group of teaching colleagues inquiring into the very idea of summaries, attempting to make the task meaningful for both themselves and their students. They are not merely administering the district's goals; they are interpreting and animating those goals for their own purposes (for instance, to help students experience the writing of summaries *as writers*, not just as students). Although the conversation begins with a district rubric, the data team quickly shifts to questions about expectations, outcomes, and genre conventions. The team turns summaries into a site of inquiry. As Angie explains, "We look at models from published writing or we look at past student work. We discuss our own expectations and write models to make sure we know what we are looking for and what we need to teach." These conversations continue until the teachers arrive at shared expectations for students' summaries. According to Angie, "These conversations take time and can often be messy. Conflicting opinions and the need for clarification are par for the course. The conversations are part of an inquiry process that is very powerful professional development."

After solidifying expectations, Angie and her colleagues gave their students a "preassessment" to determine their students' abilities to write a summary. Students read an article and wrote a summary in class. The teachers read the summaries and noted their observations of the students' writing. They then met as a team to discuss what they saw across all of the classes. "This year," Angie says,

> when we discussed the preassessment in conjunction with the scoring guide, we saw the need for explicit lessons on organizing and paraphrasing in addition to our usual lessons on finding the main idea and key details in a text. As a group, we discussed new ideas and previous lessons for teaching concepts like transitions, logical order, and ways to use an author's words in your own writing.

With a better sense of trends in her students' writing, Angie returned to her classroom, where she reviewed with students the data teams' findings, taught minilessons, and showed examples of real-world summaries.

After some classroom practice, the data team decided it was time to give a common formative assessment on summarization; see Figure 3.1 for a visual representation of how Angie moved back and forth between her classroom and her data team. Again Angie reviewed her students' writing. While she saw improvement in

Figure 3.1. Angie's inquiry–practice dialectic in graphic form.

Angie assigns a preassessment to her students. The students read an article and then write a summary.

→

Reviewing all her students' first attempts at writing a summary, Angie notices her students struggling with writing a focused main idea sentence. Also, she sees a need for practice in paraphrasing, as the bulk of the summaries are direct quotes from the article.

→

Teachers in the data team see a trend across all their classes: students need more work on main idea statements, organizing, and paraphrasing. The data team discusses interventions and lessons to help students in these areas.

After meeting with her colleagues, Angie returns to her classroom and teaches main idea sentences, summary, and paraphrasing and then provides opportunities for students to practice writing a summary before the next assessment.

→

In this round of writing summaries, Angie sees improvement in her students' gathering of important details and paraphrasing, but there is still a need for practice in writing a main idea sentence.

→

Angie meets again with her data team. After discussing their students' summaries, they revisit and clarify their expectations for main idea sentences. The data team also collaborates on a sequence of lessons to help students write stronger main idea sentences.

Angie returns to her classroom and over the next week and a half implements the strategies the data team discussed. After additional practice, students are ready for the final assessment.

→

Across her classes, Angie observes improvement in main idea statements and students' paraphrasing of the texts.

→

At the end of the summarization unit, Angie's data team is pleased with students' improvement in paraphrasing and main idea sentences; however, the teachers note future work needed in organization and the use of transitions.

gathering important details and paraphrasing, she noticed that her students needed further practice in pulling the key ideas into one cohesive main idea sentence, as called for by the rubric. In her next data team meeting, Angie shared her observations with her team. As the team discussed what they were seeing in their students' writing, they realized they needed to revisit and clarify their expectations regarding main idea sentences. Angie explains:

> When we compared student summaries on our first [pre]assessment, we did some collaborative scoring. The scoring guide required proficient summaries to begin with an accurate main idea statement, a sentence that overviewed the key ideas of the piece. The article we used for this assessment discussed the formation of the Great Barrier Reef in detail, the use of the reef for marine life, and the destruction of the reef. The five teachers scoring these summaries were accepting a wide range of main idea sentences as [acceptable], some as general as "The Great Barrier Reef is a magnificent structure." Some teachers were relieved just to get anything that sounded like an introductory sentence. Expectations were transformed, however, when someone in the group made the connection between a thesis statement for an essay and the main idea sentence of a summary. Would we accept in one of our student's essays a thesis statement that is extremely general or partial in its coverage of the key ideas in the essay? Of course, the answer was no. After this re-articulation of expectations, we went back into our classrooms and worked with students on creating main idea statements that covered the key ideas in the piece.

Based on this discussion of student work, the teachers returned to their classrooms with a new approach to assist their students. As Angie explains,

> The process was not easy, but we collaborated on a sequence of lessons that we thought would get students where we wanted them to be. We began with lessons that had students creating main idea statements for short paragraphs. We then taught students to chunk longer articles into sections, noting the primary topic or key idea in each chunk so that the main idea sentence for their summary included all of the key ideas of the longer piece.

After students had multiple opportunities to craft summaries, and with the end of the semester approaching, Angie and her colleagues gave their students a summative assessment. Once again, they gave students an article to read and asked them to write a summary. Now Angie and her colleagues could see marked improvement in the students' summaries, which were more comprehensive, detailed, and focused than their earlier efforts. At the same time, the teachers were able to identify concepts and skills they would need to return to later in the year, as well as students who needed additional practice in writing summaries.

Angie describes the benefit of inquiring into student writing with her colleagues:

A regular discussion of what we are doing with our students, how they are performing, and what steps need to be taken next is the main work of our data teams. Assessment is an ongoing process that is woven together with focused and purposeful instruction. Doing this with a small group of dedicated teachers has been a great growth opportunity for everyone involved—most importantly, our students.

At the center of the team's work is student writing. As they review their students' writing, they ask questions of themselves and one another: What do you see? What are the strengths of this piece? What are the weaknesses? How can we help more students succeed in these ways? How can we help more students avoid these problems? Moving back and forth between team meetings and their classrooms in the spirit of inquiry allows these teachers to gain the kind of adaptive expertise that is at the heart of teachers' work.

Teachers' Expertise as Practical Wisdom

Angie and her colleagues have adopted the inquiry stance within their data team: they collectively generate knowledge-in-context—or what we think of as "practical wisdom." This phrase, which we borrow from Aristotle, names a particular kind of expertise, one that applies not to narrowly technical activities but rather to adaptive arts such as teaching. According to Aristotle, practical wisdom, or *phronesis*, is a virtue of the intellect (VI, 1). It involves the ability to "deliberate well" about special cases, rather than about universals (VI, 5). Unlike philosophical wisdom, which is concerned with the gods, practical wisdom is "concerned with things human" (VI, 7) and won by experience in the world (VI, 8). Significantly, Aristotle ties practical wisdom to "good or sympathetic judgment" (VI, 11). He even suggests that "we ought to attend to the undemonstrated sayings and opinions of [the practically wise] no less than to [scientific] demonstrations; for because experience has given them an eye they see aright" (I, 11). This is a remarkable statement—especially coming from a philosopher trained in physical science! But Aristotle is saying that when thoughtful people deliberate well on their experiences, they gain not just knowledge, not only "skill," but wisdom.

Wisdom is not a word thrown around lightly these days. But we think it's important to distinguish between people who have knowledge and skills and people who have the practical wisdom to bring to bear their skills and knowledge in complex, relational work. In the case of teaching, this expertise must be used to inform not only teachers' own professional judgment but also students' abilities to deliberate well and arrive at informed judgments.

Teacher expertise, in short, is a form of practical wisdom, rooted in collective inquiry and experience, produced through careful deliberation, and resulting in considered professional judgment. It is, or should be, the cornerstone of educational decision making. Unfortunately, teacher expertise traditionally has been pushed aside, unrecognized, in favor of the designs of policymakers, politicians, and pundits. Many of these designs are motivated by arguments based on the results of standardized tests, while the judgments of the professionals who work side by side with students each day are shunted aside. The claim is that the tests are more "objective," but as the authors of the *Standards for the Assessment of Reading and Writing* observe, complex human practices such as literacy cannot be measured and reported "objectively"; for that matter, even a test score "must be interpreted, which is always a subjective and value-laden process" (8). Intriguingly, the SARW authors invite us to imagine what assessment conversations would be like if "teachers' observations were described as 'direct documentation' and test results as 'indirect estimation'" (9). This thought experiment underscores teachers' privileged positions vis-à-vis teaching and learning and puts a premium on the knowledge they produce. It stands in stark contrast to the long-honored tradition of treating teachers as passive recipients of others' expertise by requiring them to sit through talking head after talking head at mandatory inservices and trainings.

The conventional "staff development" model imports expertise from elsewhere—universities, professional organizations, staff development organizations, assessment companies, etc.—in the form of "best practices" that teachers must adopt in their classrooms. Rarely do these experts learn deeply about specific school contexts or listen to and learn from teachers. Fortunately, however, as the burgeoning of teacher research literature suggests, other models of professional development have emerged, and these feature collaborative teacher inquiry as the vehicle for developing teacher expertise. These models recognize the limits of imported expertise and the value of developing teachers' expertise as they enact the dialectic between inquiry and practice. Laura Robb, in *Redefining Staff Development*, describes these new models under the broad rubric of "professional study." Such models hold that "[w]hen teachers inquire, when they pose questions about their needs, frustrations, and hopes and continue questioning as they learn and apply new practices in their classroom, a culture of inquiry, reflection, and self-evaluation develops" (1).

Many districts have adopted collaborative inquiry structures such as data teams and professional learning communities (PLCs) that may support the development of cultures of inquiry. We say "may" because, as we learned in talking with many teachers as we worked on this book, these "professional development opportunities" often turn out to be bureaucratic structures designed solely to generate and process data (narrowly conceived as student scores) or to allow administrators to force-feed, and hold teachers accountable for, "best practices," thereby turning teachers back into passive recipients of others' expertise. In practice, for instance, the hugely popular PLCs are often highly instrumentalist, rigid, and top-down (Cochran-Smith and Lytle, *Inquiry* 59).[1] No matter the model or structure, if a "professional development" activity does not grant teachers the role of expert and allow them to develop their expertise by way of collaborative inquiry, then it is little more than a management strategy.

Angie and her colleagues show us that teachers can use these organizational structures to learn and plan together in the tradition of teacher inquiry. We hope that whenever possible, teachers exploit these structures to support the dialectic of inquiry and practice. At the same time, we hope teachers and administrators continue to develop alternative structures, processes, and relationships that support this dialectic.

Some of these activities may well involve people from outside the school walls. As Cochran-Smith and Lytle suggest in the passage we use as an epigraph to this chapter, teachers' capacity emerges when they work "collectively with one another *and with others*" (emphasis added). Indeed, as we see in the following examples, often teachers can "borrow" the expertise of these others to extend their own expertise and that of their students. By the same token, teachers—precisely because they are teachers—share what they know, both with their students and with other educational partners. This is an important feature of teachers' expertise: unlike guild knowledge—which is carefully withheld from lay people to protect the status of guild members—it is not reliant upon others *not* knowing. Teachers share not only what they know about their subjects but also what they know about learning itself. While only teachers can produce the deep, situated knowledge about learning that their ongoing inquiry provides, they deploy that knowledge toward the construction of what the SARW authors describe as "centers of inquiry where students, teachers, and other members of the school community investigate their own learning, both individually and collaboratively" (3). Teachers' professional expertise is special because—in contrast with many other professions' expertise, which is jealously hoarded and guarded—it is aimed at deepening and extending others' expertise.

It is particularly appropriate to draw on the expertise of people outside our classrooms when it comes to writing assessment, since writing constantly circulates and is evaluated outside our classrooms. Expert readers and evaluators of various kinds of texts can help teachers and students learn how to value those texts in the contexts in which audiences encounter them. Deb Title-Grove and Keith Pardeck, high school language arts teachers in Missouri, show us what this kind of collaboration might look like in a high school course devoted to workplace communication.

Deb and Keith "Borrow" Expertise: Developing Practical Wisdom

Deb and Keith were recently assigned to teach a course that was new to them: Language Communication and Composition (LCC). This course is designed to help students planning to enter the workforce directly after high school or attend a technical college to develop workplace communication competency. The district curriculum guide described the course as focusing on *workplace communication*, but Deb and Keith were unsure what this term meant, exactly. They were also uncertain about what employers in their area were looking for in new employees. This uncertainty was especially pronounced vis-à-vis writing, as Deb explains:

> When it came to writing, we had a lot more trouble looking for assessments for kids whose interests ranged from hairdressing to the military to farming to managing a Hardee's restaurant. I am not a business professional. I do not have a background working in any other career besides education, so right away I knew I would need help in the areas of modeling and assessing writing.

Because "writing" would be different for each student depending on her or his choice of career, Deb and Keith quickly realized that their expertise as teachers would need to be supplemented by the workplace expertise of small business owners, organization directors, and HR representatives in their community.

For the centerpiece of the first semester of LCC, Deb and Keith asked students to choose a career they were interested in and apply for an entry-level position with a company or organization. Specifically, students created a portfolio with the following artifacts: (1) a letter of application; (2) a professional résumé with a specific objective; (3) interview questions both general and job specific (these were created by the students to help prepare for their interviews); (4) a references page; (5) an artifact page (pictures or examples of their skills, experiences, leadership, etc.); (6) a postinterview reflection; and (7) a formal follow-up/thank you letter to the interviewer. At the end of the first semester, each student would meet with a prospective employer in the field they identified and interview for an entry-level position.

Throughout the semester, Deb and Keith invited business and organizational professionals into their classrooms to share "honorable and horrible" examples of job application materials as well as interview techniques and tips. Students also read articles in *Newsweek* and *Businessweek* about trends in the economy, and they studied and evaluated examples of the genres in which they would need to perform. For example, students studied the conventions of résumés and compared and ranked actual examples of résumés. Through this close attention to the conventions of these texts, students began to notice subtleties such as the importance of using strong verbs.

Deb and Keith also coordinated with their school's Partners in Education office, inviting potential employers to the school during finals week to interview students for an entry-level position and to review their written materials. For each interview:

1. The employer read through the student's portfolio.

2. The employer interviewed the student using some of the questions the student provided, along with others the employer typically asks.

3. After the interview, the employer switched to "mentor mode" and discussed the student's written and spoken performance and provided suggestions for improvement.

4. The employer filled out a rubric assessing the student's speaking, writing, and research skills as well as some dispositions displayed in the interview. Students were informed by the employer if they would have been offered a second interview or hired for the position or if they would not have advanced in the job search process.

5. Students watched and assessed their videotaped interviews and mentoring sessions and then wrote a reflection on the experience, documenting their strengths, weaknesses, and areas of improvement.

Many of Deb and Keith's classroom lessons were reinforced in the mentoring part of the interview. As Keith explains, "In school, students don't always understand the real-world application of word choice. The real lesson comes when someone who actually works in the field of their interest explains to them that in the workplace, there are times when word choice is really important." For instance, one of Keith's students was interviewing for a position as a firefighter with a local fire chief. The student did well with the interview portion of the project; however, when reviewing the student's written work, the fire chief mentioned that the student's word choice might have hampered his chances of making it to the interview stage. The fire chief pointed out that when the student wrote in his cover letter about his "adrenaline rush" in high-stress situations, he ran the risk of revealing not an asset, as the student intended, but rather a liability, because firefighters must stay calm and levelheaded in such situations.

Feedback from potential employers was valuable not only for students but also for Deb and Keith. Deb, for instance, learned an important lesson about professional writing:

> I learned that I need to get better teaching these genres. Most of the students had the proper format, conventions, etc. but what they lacked is the standout feature. I need to help students to demonstrate their knowledge of the content and skills required to do their job and to present that in a compelling and convincing manner to an employer. We worked hard to make sure their materials were *correct*, and they need to

be, but what was clear was that they needed to be professionally personalized for the job and company. I don't know if any of our kids would have gotten the job because you have to be better than a template. Correct is not good enough.

Deb and Keith came to realize that correct, polished prose is a necessary ingredient of workplace writing, but only one ingredient. Teaching workplace writing effectively would require them to shift from a general-skills approach to one in which students were guided—by their teachers and mentors—to develop the complex literacy practices of their chosen fields, with their purposes and audiences always in mind.

We worked hard to make sure their materials were *correct,* and they need to be, but what was clear was that they needed to be professionally personalized for the job and company. I don't know if any of our kids would have gotten the job because you have to be better than a template. Correct is not good enough.

—Deb Title-Grove

As they look forward to next year's version of LLC, Deb and Keith are planning a series of revisions to support this new conceptualization of the course. For example, they plan to provide additional mentoring support throughout the course. Although they will continue having students interview for a specific entry-level position, they will also partner each student with a mentor in the field the student is interested in but not from the company with which the student will interview. Keith stated, "I don't know if I can coach [a specific discourse] for each student. We need to find experts in the fields to help mentor our students in the content and professional discourse of writing and interviewing for a position in their field." Including a mentor throughout the semester will provide students opportunities to receive formative feedback and insight from an insider in the field as well as feedback from Deb and Keith. The teachers also plan to revise the assessment tool for potential employers. Instead of using a traditional classroom rubric with a score, they intend to create a form that solicits narrative feedback from professionals in the field. They believe this kind of feedback will be more meaningful to their students.

Deb and Keith's work on the LCC course demonstrates one way to develop assessments that solicit "multiple perspectives" (SARW Standard 8; 24), including those of community members (Standard 9; 26). While this course is a work in progress, it will continue to feature students' writing portfolios as a site in which the perspectives of students, teachers, and business and organizational professionals are triangulated. The goal is not to land students jobs—though that might happen—but rather to help students understand the importance of studying and practicing workplace discourses and genres to expand their range of possibilities and opportunities.

The triangulation that Deb and Keith have orchestrated allows them to "borrow" the expertise of others as a means of extending their own. They are more expert teachers of professional writing when they involve business and organizational professionals in engaging and assessing students' writing.[2] In our next example, Jane Percival, a middle school teacher in western Massachusetts, similarly extends her expertise by engaging students in a series of conversations with knowledgeable people inside and beyond their school. Jane's example shows how students can be both the recipients and the providers of assessment information at critical points throughout an extended project. It also shows how this work allows *students* to develop expertise, not only in their chosen subjects but also in teaching and learning.

Jane's Students Exhibit Expertise: Extending Conversations

Two large rooms, sixteen windows into the world: the physics of flight, silk in ancient China, Buddhist art, coral reef pollution and protection, equine therapy, Egyptian hieroglyphics, styles of screenwriting, ancient Greek technology, Emily Dickinson's garden and poetry, Norse and Hindu myths . . . and more. Sixteen stations, sixteen experts sharing what they know about a topic they have studied deeply and well.

The experts speak; the visitors listen. And not just that:

A parent makes a paper airplane, learning how wing design affects gliding. Kids write their names in hieroglyphics on the walls of a giant paper tomb. A teacher watches an animation of an ancient Greek protosteam engine. A crowd debates which bottle rocket design will lead to the greatest achieved height. A community member watches a movie deploying three different scriptwriting styles. A grandfather and his grandson play a board game based on the Peloponnesian War. Kids use brightly colored crayons to approximate the vivid hues of silk clothing. A group gathers to view a poetry scrapbook adorned with pressed flowers.

"Tell me about . . ."

"Do you want to hear about . . .?"

"I never knew that."

"Can you believe these kids?"

For the eighth-grade students of this small, public charter school and their families—indeed, for the entire community—this is a night of celebration. Each exhibit, the culmination of a multiphase, months-long independent research project (IRP), represents a major intellectual achievement. Each student has become an expert in her or his chosen topic. But for Jane and her fellow teacher John Van Beckum, co-creator of the IRP, the value of the project lies not so much in what students have come to know, but in how they've learned to learn. They want their students to "know their stuff," to be sure, but they also want them to take an inquiry stance: to commit themselves to the long, slow process of asking questions, gathering information, trying out ideas, asking new questions, gathering new information, trying out new ideas, etc. And perhaps above all, they want them to understand that *conversation* with a variety of knowledgeable people is at the heart of inquiry. That is why Jane and John make conversation the heart of the collaborative assessment of the IRPs.

The eighth-grade IRPs, a school graduation requirement, began in December with the identification of topics. Jane and John gave their eighth graders two parameters: the topic must be of interest to the student and it must be connected somehow to the middle school curriculum they had experienced. The teachers proposed many possible topics—hundreds, Jane says. Students brainstormed, shared lists, talked about what they knew and didn't know about their proposed topics. Their topics often shifted as their research began; Jane and John encouraged students to be focused but flexible in their thinking early on in their research.

Liam, for instance, was interested in pottery. He had taken an art class and become interested in throwing. At first, Liam thought he might study New England pottery, its history or its varieties. As he began researching this topic, however, he soon realized that he wasn't passionate about it. As he reflected on his art class and talked to Jane, who wanted to be sure his topic would sustain his interest for several months, he hit on another idea: he could study pottery in ancient Egypt. He was interested in Egypt generally, and he remembered that hieroglyphics appeared on pottery, as well as on tombs and pyramid walls. But he didn't know much about Egyptian pottery or how hieroglyphics worked in ancient Egypt. He had a lot to discover. He was off and running.

Much of students' early work on the projects revolved around the research paper. Jane first led students through activities designed to help them find sources—formulating and experimenting with search terms, learning the conventions of the library catalog and research databases, searching for local experts, etc. She then asked them simply to read about their topics: to browse the literature, in leisurely fashion, noticing what was interesting and important, but not yet taking notes. Jane believes the first step in becoming an expert is to read widely, with one's ears and eyes open but without a specific agenda—except, of course, to learn. Only after students narrowed their topic and found a foothold did they begin their note-taking. They took notes on sources for about a month, with increasing independence once Jane ensured they were tracking full bibliographic information and using summary, paraphrase, and quotation effectively.

Liam's research question evolved away from pottery per se and toward hieroglyphics themselves; he asked, "How were hieroglyphics important to ancient Egyptian society?" He became interested in the use of hieroglyphics in religious rituals and to commemorate the dead in tombs. He was also intrigued by the role and status of scribes in ancient Egypt.

While the eighth graders worked on their IRPs, Jane's seventh graders were conducting their own, more focused research projects on the Renaissance. (The integrative curricular focus for the seventh and eighth graders was the European Renaissance.) Each student chose a Renaissance figure—and Jane did the same, choosing to complete her own research project on Martin Luther. (Conducting her own research project, Jane says, reminds her of the challenges and joys of undertaking a major research project. She brings her own project through the steps that she teaches her students.) The class generated research questions together and studied Renaissance-style portraiture.

Jane and John convened the two grades after the students had created their research note cards and had tentatively assigned topical headings to the cards. Seventh and eighth graders were paired and, with their cards spread out on the floor, together they explored possible arrangements of information for their respective research papers. Over two days, the students served as each other's writing consultants, getting and giving feedback on their emerging projects. This was an important assessment moment for students, as they learned not only how to use feedback they got from colleagues but also how to read their own work critically as they engaged with the work of their peers.

Once students arrived at tentative research paper outlines, they had a focused conversation with their advisor (Jane or John) in which they shared what they had learned and began discussing the best ways to represent that learning in an exhibit, which would take place at the end of the spring semester. Before they could move forward with plans for their exhibit, they had to convince their advisor that they had developed expertise in their chosen topic. While this feedback came from a teacher, not a peer, those teachers took on the role of advisors because they wanted students to receive advice from multiple perspectives and make judicious decisions about their next steps.

These meetings were also opportunities for students to receive oral feedback on their research papers. Jane and John used basic rubrics—"perhaps more checklists, really," Jane says—to help students understand the components of strong research writing. Jane is a proponent of simple rubrics. "If a rubric gets too detailed," she says, "it gets in the way." Besides, she adds, "rubrics are evaluative, and that's not what helps students move forward. But they are a way to start a conversation, especially when they provide opportunities for teachers or peers to write a comment or a question, rather than just check boxes. The one-on-one meetings I have with students are most important." For Jane, rubrics are occasional evaluative check-ins; the conversations she has with her students, on the other hand, are continual.

In addition to these advisory meetings with their teacher, students met with teachers other than their own. First, toward the end of the spring semester, they presented their research to a faculty committee. The purpose of this meeting was for students to demonstrate that they could converse knowledgeably about their topic. They were to take up the expert role and share what they knew with the committee members. Students set up drafts of their exhibit boards and any other technologies they planned to use during the exhibit. The presentations to the faculty committee were not as formal as the exhibits—they were more conversational—but they were conceived as opportunities to receive feedback on how to improve the presentation of material. The faculty asked questions and provided oral feedback to students and offered written feedback to the student's teacher. Also, very close to the exhibit date, students had one more in-depth, one-on-one consultation with one teacher who was not their own to help them fine-tune their exhibits.

[Students] know what matters.

—Jane Percival

In addition, throughout the process students worked with mentors in the community. Early in the research process, Jane and John helped students identify and contact local experts in their topics—professionals, practitioners, and scholars who had firsthand knowledge—who could meet occasionally with students on a volunteer basis to advise them as they developed their projects. Liam, for instance, first worked with a local potter and then, as his project evolved from pottery to hieroglyphics, switched to an anthropology professor at a nearby college. The professor helped Liam better understand Egyptian culture and artifacts and advised him on the design of his exhibit. The mentors represent another interlocutor, in addition to teachers and peers, from whom students get response, conversation, and resources. Jane and John also gather feedback from mentors about their experiences with students through a questionnaire; this feedback informs both how they advise their students and how they continue to develop the IRP curriculum.

Finally, a couple of weeks before the exhibit, Jane and John convened all the eighth graders to form a support group as they made final preparations for their exhibits. They also again partnered the eighth graders with seventh graders so the latter could provide response to and suggestions for the exhibit plans. (This practice also allowed the seventh graders to begin thinking about their own eighth-grade IRPs.)

Like Deb and Keith, Jane and John seek to provide students with multiple perspectives on their evolving projects. At key points throughout the year, students received a wealth of formative responses to and advice about their in-process work. As the end of spring semester approached, Jane and John helped students sort through all the feedback they'd received. One important strategy was to review the written journals students had kept throughout the project. This allowed students to consider the array of advice they had received along the way and to choose which advice to follow as they prepared their final exhibits.

Meanwhile, Jane also involved students in developing a rubric to evaluate the final exhibits. This was important to her because she wanted students to take ownership of their projects—and because it allowed her to check, consolidate, and extend students' understanding of the projects. For instance, Jane and John had decided that the exhibits would be interactive, using media and genres of students' choice (a painting or piece of pottery, a musical composition, a short play, a video, an installation piece, a demonstration of a scientific experiment, an original comic book, and so on). When they discussed this issue of medium as they worked on the rubric, students insisted that while the use of various technologies is appropriate for the exhibits, exhibitors should carefully integrate technologies only when the information could not be presented effectively without using them. They did not want exhibitors to use technologies only for the "wow factor." They also insisted that the use of technology should not extend the length of an individual exhibit in a way that would deter visitors from seeing the other exhibits. The idea, students determined, was to offer audiences—teachers, their families, and community members—an *experience* of the topic that would be meaningful and memorable. According to Jane, this kind of insight is typical of her students; "they know what matters," she insists. They were coming to know not only about their research topics but also about how to teach and learn about those topics.

Students indeed used a wide variety of technologies in their exhibits; they created PowerPoint presentations, websites, movies and documentaries, animations, models, scrapbooks, and more. They displayed the wide range of "literacies" we discussed in Chapter 1, carefully weighing the affordances and limitations of various media and modalities. Liam's exhibit was low-tech but multimodally rich: he created a replica of an Egyptian tomb, pitching a tent and using large pieces of paper to make the walls. Low lighting approximated the "feel" of a typical tomb. He hoped to depict how hieroglyphics were used in religious and funerary contexts. Liam invited visitors to write their names in hieroglyphics on the walls, supplying them with a key. As he explained in his final reflection, he ran into some trouble: because very young children would be in attendance, "I was not allowed to put a coffin in the tomb." But he quickly came up with an alternative: "So instead, I created a tomb antechamber for riches and gold." Like his classmates, Liam developed an exhibit that appealed to younger and older visitors. The kids were so fond of writing on the tomb walls, in fact, that Liam had to replace the paper.

As for the exhibit boards, the 4-point rubric Jane and her students developed was comprehensive. It covered

- the process of putting the boards together ("had necessary materials; engaged assistance of 7th grader; followed stated directions; solved problems efficiently; met production deadlines");

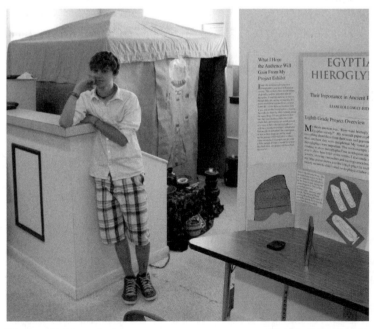

Liam outside his tomb.   Photo by John Bidwell.

- the quality of the writing ("develops the topic; is clear to the reader; is well edited; holds the interest of the reader");

- the effectiveness of the layout/design ("use of design elements: color, shape, line, mass, and texture—so that audience attention is gained; design elements work together; project topic is communicated; a 'page architecture' is evident"); and

- the quality of the displayed elements ("paper/photos trimmed accurately; elements secured with glue, tape, etc.; backing attached so as not to be distracting; clear images on photos").

Again, for Jane, the evaluative nature of the rubrics is less important than the way they enable conversations with students about the nature of the work. In this instance, she was primarily interested in working with students on the multimodal composing of their boards—especially the way their compositions combined textual and visual elements. Jane and her students also developed criteria by which to assess the quality of the individual written pieces that constituted the board: a paragraph describing the project, a reflective journal entry on "What I Hope the Audience Will Gain from My Project Exhibit," a reflective paragraph on "How My Journal Illustrates My Eighth-Grade Project Journey," and an informational sketch of the student's project mentor.

Formal and informal forms of writing assessment are woven throughout the eighth-grade IRP. Jane and John have designed the project so that students have consistent opportunities throughout to converse with a range of interlocutors: seventh- and eighth-grade peers, teachers, mentors, and family and community members. Clearly, they take seriously the principle of Standard 8 of the IRA–NCTE *Standards for the Assessment of Reading and Writing*: that "the assessment process should involve multiple perspectives and sources of data" (24). Their work also illustrates how families can become "involved as active, essential participants in the assessment process," as recommended by Standard 11 (29). Indeed, community members and families are not mere spectators of the projects; the rubric for the exhibit states that the exhibit itself must "support the audience member in informing the exhibitor about what s/he has learned about the project from doing the interactive element." Conversation is built into the exhibit rubric.

To *converse*, of course, means to engage in a reciprocal discussion, a back-and-forth. But it also means to keep company and to render familiar (as in "be conversant in"). Although this project is termed "independent," it's clear that Jane and her colleagues agree with Cochran-Smith and Lytle that independence of mind and sound judgment—the kind we normally associate with "experts"—comes only through keeping good company with a range of knowledgeable others. For them, writing assessment—whether it involves an oral discussion, a panel, a checklist, or

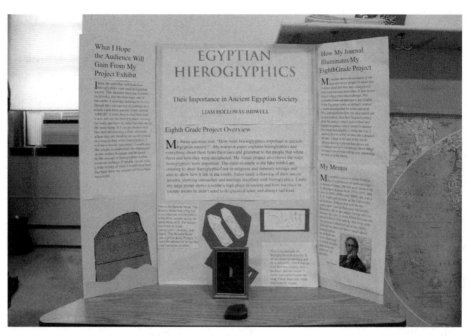

Liam's exhibit board.   Photo by John Bidwell

a rubric—is an opportunity to give and receive response to an ongoing and person-ally meaningful writing project.

———————

At Jane's suggestion, we offer a brief postscript to her story: Just as she asks her students to revise their work over time, so Jane and John revise the eighth-grade indepen-dent project each year. They redraft the mentor letters, revise the rubrics based on interactions and conversations with each year's students, and add new elements to the curriculum. In the version of the project described here, for instance, Jane and John spent much more time than in previous years helping students find topics that would sustain their interest over the several months of the project. This deci-sion was prompted by previous instances in which some students lost interest after committing too early to a topic. And every year, Jane and John do all of this very quickly, completing their preparations—again, much like their students—in the nick of time. "I do the best I can do at this moment," Jane says. "I know I'll revise it again."

Why is this important to note? "Because," Jane offers, "I wouldn't want your readers to think it's perfect or has to be perfect. What I've learned is you just put your toe in the water; at least you're starting to get wet."

Jane's advice reminds us that inquiry and expertise go hand in hand. We tend to think of expertise as the outcome of inquiry—the place, perhaps, where it stops. Inquiry is the means; expertise is the end. But notice that in each of the examples in this chapter—indeed, in all of our chapters—the teachers *continue* to engage in inquiry, even as they achieve considerable expertise. Angie and her colleagues continue to search for ways to use their data team to inquire into student writing; Deb and Keith continue to build the curriculum for Language Communication and Composition; Jane and John continue to develop the Independent Research Project. This is so not because they aren't happy with these experiences, but rather because they understand that teaching is an adaptive art that requires continuous inquiry. These teachers know that educational experiences can never be perfected and replicated but that they *can* be shaped and guided by the practical wisdom won from inquiry into them and into previous experiences. This is what teachers know how to do: to inquire into irreducibly complex and dynamic teaching and learning situations; to engage others—students, community members, parents—as co-inquirers; and to use that inquiry to support teaching and learning in schools and beyond them. This expertise cannot be codified or commodified; it must be earned through deep, continuous engagement in the hard work of teaching and learning.

This expertise that only teachers can develop should be a source of considerable authority in the development and implementation of policies and practices that promote effective teaching and learning. To be sure, other educational partners—including and especially students—have expertise of their own to contribute, as we have seen in this chapter. These forms of expertise should augment the practical wisdom of teachers, informing our better judgment. As the authors of the *Standards for the Assessment of Reading and Writing* imply, and as we have shown throughout this chapter, there is no contradiction between the claim that the teachers' judgment is paramount in assessment (Standard 2) and the suggestion that assessment should solicit and learn from the perspectives of various others, including parents, community members, and other educational partners (Standards 8–11). But as teachers, we must make plain what educational policymakers too often "forget": that our expertise is irreplaceable; that our professional judgment is indispensible; and that, as a result, our leadership is critical. This last claim is the focus of the next chapter.

Notes

1. PLCs are wildly popular—as a quick search using any Internet search engine will demonstrate—but, like data teams, they have become controversial among teachers. Defenders of PLCs such as Shirley Hord and Richard DuFour claim that PLCs ought to be focused on student learning and teacher inquiry and collaboration, and DuFour argues that PLCs are not always practiced with fealty to that vision (DuFour; Hord; DuFour and

Eaker). Many teachers, however, describe PLCs as Trojan horses for common assessments and claim that PLCs have no positive impact on their teaching. See, for instance, Maja Wilson's comments in Chapter 4.

2. While we encourage teachers to turn to professionals in their communities for expertise and partnership, as Deb and Keith did, we should note that there are significant literatures on technical and professional communication, workplace and community writing, and writing across the curriculum. These may also prove to be valuable resources for teacher inquiry. For an interesting and important statement about reading and writing across the curriculum in the context of the Common Core State Standards Initiative, see NCTE's *Reading and Writing Across the Curriculum: A Policy Research Brief.*

Practicing Writing Assessment Leadership

Until the public school system is organized in such a way that every teacher has some regular and representative way in which he or she can register judgment upon matters of educational importance, with the assurance that this judgment will somehow affect the school system, the assertion that the present system is not, from the internal standpoint, democratic seems justified. Either we come here upon some fixed and inherent limitation upon the democratic principle, or else we find in this fact an obvious discrepancy between the conduct of the school and the conduct of social life—a discrepancy so great as to demand immediate and persistent effort at reform.

—John Dewey, "Democracy in Education" (195)

I n this final chapter, we shift the focus from writing assessment expertise to writing assessment leadership. In doing so, we join a chorus of researchers and scholars who assert that the key to meaningful school improvement lies in building communities of teacher leaders who spark school change "from the inside out" (Elmore; see also Darling-Hammond; Deal and Peterson; Gallagher, *Reclaiming*; Hargreaves, Earl, Moore, and Manning; Sergiovanni; Westheimer). We join Michael Fullan, who suggests in *Change Forces* that "teaching will not become a learning profession until the vast majority of its members become . . . change agents capable of working on their own sense of purpose, through inquiry, competence building, and collaboration" (127). We join Roland S. Barth, who in his book *Learning by Heart* writes, "[I]f schools are going to become places where all children and adults are learning in worthy ways, all teachers *must* lead" (85, emphasis in original). We join Cathy Fleischer, who in *Teachers Organizing for Change* writes that teachers "must become leaders in informing the public about the complexity and the reality of public education" (6).

At the same time, our call for teacher leadership for writing assessment builds on the critical foundation set by the IRA–NCTE *Standards for the Assessment of Reading and Writing* (SARW). Throughout this book, we have identified Standard 2—"The teacher is the most important agent of assessment"—as a key challenge and opportunity for teachers (13). To meet this challenge, we have argued, teachers must develop their assessment literacy (Chapter 2) and their assessment expertise (Chapter 3). We have underscored in particular the role of teachers' professional *judgment*. As the authors of the SARW suggest, teachers "cannot defer [judgment] to others or to other instruments" (14). Teachers are uniquely positioned to make educational judgments about students and to use those judgments to help them improve as writers (and readers). In this chapter, we extend these arguments to suggest that all the assessment literacy and expertise in the world will not be enough if teachers do not exert *leadership* that places their professional judgment at the center of the educational enterprise.[1]

This point was driven home to us as we began work on this chapter, which would turn out to be by far the most difficult chapter to write. In fact, we wondered at times if we could write it at all. For although we were joining a robust chorus of calls for teacher leadership, it proved exceedingly difficult to *find* teacher-leaders to feature in the chapter.

Sure, we knew some teachers who had been tapped by their schools, districts, or states to serve on committees or to facilitate top-down assessment processes. But it soon became clear, in talking with these colleagues, that they were often treated as "token teachers"; they lent legitimacy to the process, but their participation was more symbolic than substantive. In fact, most of these teachers felt betrayed by such experiences and regretted having participated. Among those who didn't feel this way, the prevailing sentiment was one of resignation: they said, in effect, "The state/district assessment is what it is; I might as well be the first to know." This is of course not what we had in mind when we went in search of teacher-leaders for writing assessment. We were—and are—interested in teachers who helped *shape* assessment policy and practice, rather than those who only facilitated the process on behalf of administrators or policymakers.

As we reached out to colleagues near and far, however, exchanges such as the following turned out to be far more common:[2]

Hey J.,

Eric and I are still looking for teachers who have helped shape assessment policy and practice beyond their individual schools. We're looking for activist-teachers to feature—folks who aren't just "involved" in district or state initiatives but who have really pushed for meaningful, authentic writing assessment for (or—imagine!—with) kids and have something, no matter how minor, to show for it. Any ideas?

Chris

Hi Chris,

Hmmm, good question. No one springs immediately to mind. I wonder if I even know anyone who fits your description. I mean, if the district or the state accepts an approach to assessment, it's probably not what I would call meaningful! I know a lot of teachers who are spending a lot of time resisting stupid ideas coming from their districts and states, but usually the best they can do is create a little bit of space where they can do some work very locally. They're not really "shaping policy and practice," though. At best, they're escaping top-down policies and practices to do something meaningful and authentic. Probably not what you had in mind. I'll keep thinking and will let you know if I come up with any ideas.

J.

Sometimes the response was even less promising:

Chris and Eric,

I shared your query with my network of local teachers. We just don't have anyone who is doing anything right now that fits the bill. Because of the economic collapse and state budget deficit, the district is closing some schools and reorganizing the central office. These teachers are worried about having jobs next year. One teacher, who has been writing about assessment, has been working to resist the mindless weekly comprehension tests that fourth-graders have to take. For his very thoughtful critique, he got transferred to a different school and "demoted" to third grade (which isn't a testing grade). We are working with our senator, but our state has adopted the Common Core standards even after our teachers worked for two years with the state Department of Education to develop an interesting set of new standards. And just today, we received news that the president signed the continuing resolution that eliminates the National Writing Project from the federal budget.

Depressing.

L.

With our colleague "Beth," we thought we'd hit the jackpot. For the past three years, Beth told us, her high school had invested time and resources to partner with the local National Writing Project (NWP) site for an embedded institute. Over the summer, her administrators had asked her to spearhead a teacher-led schoolwide writing assessment project. The administration wanted to track data on writing as part of their school improvement goals and to use it for accreditation. Beth had begun to imagine the work she would need to do over the course of the school year: build alliances with faculty members, provide professional development resources for her colleagues, create an instrument that could be used across the curriculum and that fit with her schools' curriculum goals, determine a process to report and share data, etc. Her administration pledged to provide time for this work during staff development days over the school year.

Beth's excitement was short-lived, however. Fall came and went, and writing assessment was pushed off the school's agenda to make room for other priorities. In January, without warning, the same administrators who had tapped Beth to facilitate the writing assessment decided that a teacher-led project was too much work and would take too long to build from the ground up. During the two nights of parent–teacher conferences, while the teachers were meeting with parents the administrators met alone and developed a writing rubric. They then charged the English teachers with teaching the rubric to the rest of the staff. There was no discussion about the purpose of the assessment or the kinds of data that would be useful to the school. Instead, on a staff development day in February, the faculty met to look at the rubric and one example of student writing for "practice." The whole staff spent the next two and a half hours scoring more than 300 pieces of student writing. (Each piece was scored analytically by trait; some but not all of the pieces were double scored.)

The administrators were elated that they were able to produce and collect schoolwide data so quickly. In fact, one of them sent an email the evening of the scoring session that we reproduce here with minor changes to protect the privacy of those involved:

> To All Staff:
> Here is some data for you . . .
> T. started the "training" at 1:30 today. I am sending this email to you at 4:50.
> As a staff . . . you graded **305 bluebooks**.
>> The average total score was 14.33 (out of 30 possible)
>> The average total Ideas and Content was 2.48
>> The average total Organization was 2.49
>> The average total Voice was 2.56
>> The average total Word Choice was 2.29
>> The average total Sentence Fluency was 2.23
>> The average total Conventions was 2.29.
> I think this is incredible that we accomplished this work as a staff in just over 3 hours. Thanks to all of you.

There is no indication anywhere in Beth's story that this process would be good for kids—students don't enter into the equation at all. Teachers enter into it only as cogs in a data-generating machine. Nor is there any indication that administrators, teachers, or students could *learn* from this process. The school had completed the minimum requirement for writing assessment and could now move on to other, more important things. "This happens," Beth said, "because writing assessment is not a priority."

While there may be widespread agreement in reform literature that practitioners must lead the way in school improvement, the reality in many schools and districts is that teachers feel under siege: subject to top-down edicts, disenfranchised from core school activities, and fearful for their livelihoods. Educational austerity—combined with the push for externally mandated curriculum, instruction, and assessment represented by the Common Core State Standards Initiative and the assessment consortia (see Chapter 1)—has led to professional retrenchment: an all-too-understandable drawing in and drawing back by teachers whose only reasonable option (other than giving in to despair, perhaps, and leaving the profession) seems to be to play it safe.

Indeed, teachers have become a political punching bag in the national media. In Wisconsin, Governor Scott Walker's anti-union Budget Repair Bill, which strips workers (including teachers) of their right to collective bargaining, sparked numerous protests and a high-profile walkout by Democratic state legislators. In much of the media coverage of this and other events, teachers have become scapegoats—emblems of lazy, selfish, overpaid public employees living easy off the public dole. There can be little doubt that the firestorm in Wisconsin, coming as it did after almost a decade of teacher-unfriendly federal policy under the No Child Left Behind legislation, contributed to the widespread siege mentality among teachers.

Still, we must recognize that teachers have always led—through the darkest of days, into the bravest of new worlds—and they continue to do so today. We should draw strength from historical traditions of teacher leadership. Consider, for instance, nineteenth-century African American women educators, including the following:

- Charlotte Forten (1837–1914), the first African American teacher to travel to the South to teach former slaves; began teaching on St. Helena Island, South Carolina, in 1862;

- Mary Jane Patterson (1840–1894), born into slavery, the first black woman to graduate with a four-year degree from an established US college (Oberlin, 1862); began teaching in Virginia in 1864, thereafter becoming a women's rights activist and a founding member of the Colored Women's League of Washington, DC;

- Mary McLeod Bethune (1875–1955), child of former slaves, founded in 1904 the Daytona Normal and Industrial Institute for Negro Girls (now Bethune-Cookman University); was a leader in the black women's club movement, president of the National Association of Colored Women, vice president of the NAACP, and consultant to President Roosevelt.

These African American women chose to devote themselves to teaching and leading during the era of slavery, Civil War, antiliteracy laws, Jim Crow, lynchings, and disenfranchisement for African Americans and women—dark days indeed. Their legacy of education and literacy for freedom inspired later generations of teachers, such as those at Myles Horton's Highlander Folk School and Septima Clark's Citizenship Schools, which played such a pivotal role during the Civil Rights Movement in facilitating African Americans' literacy and voting rights in response to literacy requirements at the polls (see Horton; Gallagher, "Educating" for a discussion of Highlander-model leadership applied to teachers).

Moreover, communities and networks of teacher-leaders *are* emerging today (see Lieberman and Miller). Consider, for instance, the Teacher Leaders Network (TLN), an initiative of the Center for Teaching Quality (www.teacherleaders .org/home). The TLN is an online community of hundreds of teacher-leaders who convene to share their expertise and encourage one another's participation in school reform. It emerged from the vision of the Institute for Educational Leadership's 2001 report, *Leadership for Student Learning: Redefining the Teacher as Leader*, which argued that teachers are a powerful but often underutilized resource for school reform leadership. The TLN offers a range of forums and resources for teacher-leaders, including blogs, a digital library, and an online newsroom. One of its recent efforts, the New Millennium Initiative, aims to train a new generation of teacher-leaders by connecting them with other teachers, researchers, reformers, administrators, union leaders, policymakers, parents, and community members.

We have also seen the emergence of teacher leadership on the issue of assessment in particular. For instance, Horace (Rog) Lucido (author of the recent book *Educational Genocide: A Plague on Our Children*) and Joseph Lucido spearhead Educators and Parents Against Testing Abuse (EPATA), a grassroots organization that organizes protest events, runs workshops, maintains an active blog and listserv, and holds an annual conference. The Lucidos began EPATA in 2003–4 to raise awareness of the negative impacts of high-stakes standardized testing on teaching and learning. One of the organization's goals is to empower teachers to "voic[e] their opinions about high stakes testing" and to encourage legislators to "value the expertise and concerns of parents and teachers" (Educators and Parents Against Testing Abuse). Of particular concern to Joe Lucido, a fifth-grade teacher in California, is the eroding autonomy of teachers, especially in "underperforming schools," which are often underfunded and comprise mainly poor students, students of color, and students whose first or strongest language is not English. Lucido notes that in his school, which ranks high on California's Academic Performance Index (API) based on its standardized test scores, he is able to offer his young writers a robust workshop approach in which students peer review and have one-on-one conferences with their teacher. In schools with lower API rankings, teachers and students do not have the time or curricular flexibility to conduct workshops; they are forced into direct instruction and a scripted curriculum. It is especially critical for these schools, according to Lucido, that teachers and parents band together to fight testing abuse and argue for rich, engaging writing instruction and assessment (J. Lucido).

A teacher leadership organization that focuses specifically on writing is the National Writing Project (NWP). The mission of the NWP, according to its website, is to focus "the knowledge, expertise, and leadership of our nation's educators on sustained efforts to improve writing and learning for all learners." The NWP currently operates more than 200 sites in all fifty states, the District of Columbia, Puerto Rico, and the Virgin Islands, as well as two associated international sites. Among its core principles is the notion that "[t]eachers at every level—from kindergarten through college—are the agents of reform." Thus, the network places enormous emphasis on teacher leadership, both by creating teacher-leaders through its professional development offerings and by conducting research on teacher leadership in practice (see www.nwp.org/cs/public/print/resource_topic/teacher_leadership). Publications such as Shanton, McKinney, Meyer, and Friedrich's report "Composing Literacy Leadership in Professional Development" and Lieberman and Friedrich's article "Teachers, Writers, Leaders" (which appeared in the journal *Educational Leadership*) demonstrate the pervasiveness of teacher leadership for writing and show what it looks like in practice. Lieberman and Friedrich, for example, draw on a large "vignette study" to show how teacher-leaders in the NWP network create and sustain learning and leading communities by, among other things, addressing problems collectively, creating forums for shared learning, celebrating others' success, and navigating school cultures.[3]

Teachers have stepped forward to provide leadership for writing assessment at the state and local levels as well. For example, in Illinois, a group of nine teachers has advocated publicly for the implementation of a portfolio-based writing assessment system to replace the current timed essay–based system. In an article published in the *Illinois English Bulletin*, these teachers use their assessment literacy and expertise to provide a comprehensive and accessible critique of the current state tests, pointing out that the tests do not map to state writing goals and that they "drive us away from best practices in the teaching of writing and toward mastery of formulaic, superficial, and chiefly irrelevant writing tasks" (Spangler et al. 14). The teachers then propose a redesign of the system that would make use of writing portfolios, describing the benefits of such a system and providing a financial analysis of the proposed shift. This is, in short, a savvy, brave, and inspiring document. Imploring their fellow teachers to reach out to their legislators, the authors write, "Effective reform will not come—and has never come—from a top-down mandate. It will begin at the grassroots level: one classroom, one department, one school, one district at a time" (25). These teachers envision and call for writing assessment and educational reform that rely on "the professional knowledge, understanding, and judgments of Illinois writing professionals [teachers]" (26). Though the struggle for what the group calls "rigorous, valid, and fair" assessment continues in Illinois, this effort both joins our call for and enacts teacher leadership for writing assessment.

It is clear, then, that teachers *are* leading through dark days—as teachers always have. They are joining together in groups, networks, and organizations to make their voices heard. At the same time, as we have suggested, too many teachers are shrinking from claiming their assessment expertise and exerting assessment leadership. Indeed, many teachers are in full retreat in the face of the aggressive antiteacher "accountability" campaign, just waiting to see what the Common Core State Standards Initiative and the assessment consortia will bring.

This retrenchment is understandable, for reasons we discussed in Chapter 1. But something else is going on here, too: teachers' chronic underestimation of the power and quality of their judgment—and therefore their leadership potential—especially when it comes to assessment. Many teachers are quick to accept that assessment is "beyond them," and even when they do feel knowledgeable, they tend to be pessimistic about their chances for shaping assessment policy and practice. In short, many teachers find it difficult to warm up to words like *assessment* and *leadership*—terms that seem to name things *other people* do. Teachers see themselves as responding to the decisions of assessment experts and leaders rather than as *being* assessment experts and leaders.

Kathie Marshall, one of the teachers we introduce you to in this chapter, puts it well: "So many teachers feel powerless. We need to activate their voice." Interestingly, though, Kathie is far from the firebrand this line might suggest. Indeed, this middle school teacher and former literacy coach remains reluctant to adopt the mantle of "leader"—and especially "writing assessment leader." And yet, as we understand that term, she has been just that. In fact, the story of Kathie's leadership in writing assessment is the story of coming to recognize herself as a leader in the first place.

Kathie Becomes an Accidental Writing Assessment Leader: Learning and Leading Together

Kathie never meant to be a leader. She never thought of herself as leadership material. She liked working as part of a team and wasn't directive. She saw herself as a calm, easygoing team player, far from the assertive, serious school leaders she knew.

But throughout her thirty-seven-year career, Kathie has found herself repeatedly coaxed into leadership roles by her peers and supervisors. "Little by little," she says, "I was pushed into leadership . . . and I finally realized, maybe I *am* a leader." Over the years, Kathie has served as team leader and department chair, organized initiatives and teacher groups, led her literacy coach cadre, coordinated grant projects, participated in her district's teacher evaluation team, attended ongoing roundtable discussions organized by her state senator, developed professional development programs, presented at local and national conferences, written articles and reports for local and national publications, been interviewed by a national education website, attended national education seminars, and participated in the national Teacher Leaders Network. So why has she been so reluctant to apply the term *leader* to herself?

For most of her career, Kathie says, she would "just do things the way I thought I should do them." She was "not a horn blower." She joined most of the previously listed projects because she wanted to *learn* about them, not to *lead* them. Sure, she thought her perspective as a literacy coach and classroom teacher might be of value; but equally important, she wanted to be part of a team that was thinking through hard problems together.

Slowly, Kathie has come to recognize that leaders don't need to blow their own horns; they can be (as she is) "low-key and collaborative." In fact, now, she says, she believes "every teacher deserves a chance to develop leadership, including [participating in] decisions about district, state, or national policies." Tellingly, though, Kathie has been particularly reluctant to claim her leadership for writing assessment. Only recently, she says, has she come to realize that she's "pushed writing assessment all along." She explains: "I call it writing to learn; I call it teaching writing. I am constantly assessing as a teacher and teaching others how to assess, but I don't tend to focus on *assessment* as a concept." Consider, for example, Kathie's story of her work spearheading what would become a districtwide focus on teaching revision:

District 2 of Los Angeles Unified School District had recently instituted literacy cadres, and as a newly minted literacy coach, Kathie was delighted to bring together colleagues from various schools to examine their practice. Initial discussion with these colleagues revealed a general unease with teaching revision. Kathie quickly realized that some of these teachers conflated revision with editing. So the group decided to devote the year to exploring revision. Everyone in the cadre began researching various methods for teaching revision. When they met again, they all brought to the group versions of a familiar revision checklist to use with students. This checklist was useful for suggesting and tracking revision, but the teachers realized it didn't help them teach revision.

Meanwhile, as it happened, Kathie was asked to review a new book for the Teacher Leaders Network, Kelly Gallagher's Teaching Adolescent Writers. *In this book, Kathie found just the kinds of teaching strategies she and her colleagues had been looking for. (Kathie's review can be found at www.teacherleaders.org/node/154.) She shared these strategies with her colleagues and the group met for lesson study. Kathie describes the process this way:*

> *Teachers tried various strategies of Gallagher's and then brought student samples to our common planning time and/or literacy cadre meetings so we could go over the results. Individual teachers made decisions about which strategies to use and in what order, depending upon the grade and skill levels of their students. For example, . . . some of the eighth grade teachers dove straight into "STAR" (substitute, take things out, add, rearrange), which we sixth grade teachers thought was an overwhelming amount of information for our students. ESL teachers particularly liked the "question flood" because it seemed to open up the dam to allow their students to develop some fluency in their writing. Whatever the process, we tried out various strategies to see how they worked, talked about them over student work samples, and then revisited the strategy or moved on to another.*

Teachers in her schools, including ESL teachers, began reporting increased motivation and achievement among their students. "Everyone," Kathie says, was "making significant progress in writing improvement."

Emboldened, Kathie drew on the group's experience to develop a revision packet to provide support for the teaching of revision. At the end of that year, District 2 literacy cadres met for a gallery walk to share action research projects. Kathie's cadre explained their process and shared copies of the revision strategies packet. Many of these colleagues wanted a copy of the packet, so it went out to all secondary English teachers in the local district.

For Kathie, this story is about many things: leadership, professional development, collaboration, and of course teaching writing. Only recently has she come to recognize that it is also about writing assessment. When she and her colleagues gathered student writing, analyzed that writing, and then planned instruction as a result, they were engaged in writing assessment. Because this process didn't include the collection of "hard data" or involve systematic school-, district- or state-based testing, Kathie did not think of it as involving assessment at all. But now she considers this kind of work not only "assessment" but also a powerful antidote to externally imposed assessments that Kathie and her colleagues find much less useful for teaching and learning.

> District-mandated formative assessments, state-mandated summative assessments, or other externally directed data-gathering initiatives just don't pack the wallop that collaboratively developed instruction and assessment do.
>
> —Kathie Marshall

Indeed, this is the argument of an article Kathie published in *Teacher Magazine* in 2009. Earlier that year, Kathie had been invited to attend a symposium in Washington, DC, sponsored by the Alliance for Excellent Education. There she found herself surrounded by a raft of administrators and professional development "experts" (and one first-year Teach for America teacher) who had convened to discuss "data-driven school improvement." Symposium participants agreed that data are best used for supporting student achievement, not merely for compliance. But as Kathie emphasized in her contributions to the conversation, the data provided by mandated, externally imposed assessments—even if they are labeled "formative"—often are not useful to classroom teachers. As Kathie wrote in her article, "District-mandated formative assessments, state-mandated summative assessments, or other externally directed data-gathering initiatives just don't pack the wallop that collaboratively developed instruction and assessment do" (K. Marshall 2). For Kathie, "data-driven instruction and assessment" are effective only when carried out by "groups of teachers working together on data inquiry and action research" (2). Teachers must be intimately involved in gathering, analyzing, and using assessment information for it to have lasting effects for teaching and learning.

Kathie ends her *Teacher Magazine* article with a commitment to fostering her own leadership and a poignant call for other teachers to join her:

> In my developing role as a teacher leader, I do hope to have more voice in discussions about teaching and learning. This opportunity to spend a day with people who help shape national education policy was an important step in that direction for me. Stakeholders at every level need to understand the complexity of our role and support the valuable work of being "just a teacher." And it's really up to teachers, in the end, to make sure they understand. (2)

Kathie has come to embrace her role as teacher-leader for assessment, however reluctantly, out of a sense of personal and professional obligation. After three and a half decades as a teacher, she says, she is newly energized, newly motivated:

> What drives me now is a sense of urgency to lead teacher-driven initiatives because I'm so concerned about demoralization among teachers across the country and their

sense that they have no power. I'm worried about who would want to replace me after I retire because of how this beloved profession of mine is maligned in the media. I'm trying to act as a leader and a role model to other teachers by participating in policy decisions at the district and state level in order to bring teacher perspectives to the table.

The Practice of Leadership

We find Kathie to be an inspiring teacher-leader—not because of exceptional personal characteristics or skills she possesses (though she's a special person with many admirable skills), but because of the humble, everyday way she engages in the *practice* of leadership. For her, and for us, leadership is not a romantic, mystified concept. Leaders need not act alone, standing out from the crowd as extraordinarily charismatic, articulate, or vocal. And they need not always be decisive, ever aware of the right things to do at the right time, especially in moments of crisis. Finally, they need not occupy lofty positions of power at the top of an organizational chart.

It will not surprise you to learn that we think of leadership in an *inquiry* framework. This means that leaders are learners and that leadership is rooted in learning. This is an unusual way to think about leadership: we tend to think of leaders as people who have already learned how to do things and have blazed a trail for others to follow. But we agree with leadership expert Ron Heifetz, who writes that "[r]ather than define leadership either as a position of authority in a social structure or as a personal set of characteristics, we may find it a great deal more useful to define leadership as an *activity*" (20, emphasis in original). And that activity, according to Heifetz, is "mobilizing people to tackle tough problems" (15). Notice: a leader doesn't step forward to solve people's problems; a leader helps mobilize people to solve their own problems.

A leader engages in what Heifetz calls "adaptive work": work required by situations that take us beyond the familiar and comfortable, when we can no longer call on reliable routines. (Readers familiar with Donald Schön's work will hear echoes here of his "reflective practice." As we discussed in Chapter 3, teachers are often in this zone of uncertainty, dealing as we do with the irreducibly complex activities of human teaching and learning.) Leaders leverage relationships for collaborative effort, bringing people together to work on and work out shared questions and problems. They need not have an official position of authority; leaders are leaders by virtue of their actions.

For teachers, the practice of leadership can take many forms: starting a service-learning program, educating adults in the community on important educational matters, advocating for social policies that improve students' educational opportunities, helping form community alliances, writing to or meeting with politicians and policymakers, becoming active in professional organizations, writing for professional publication, forming a teacher inquiry group, etc. Though many of these activities require some political courage, practicing leadership need not be confined to strictly political activities designed to promote policy fixes (Fleischer).

> ### Assessment Leadership in an Inquiry Framework
>
> - Be a lead learner, not a lead knower
> - Practice adaptive work
> - Collaborate
> - Organize
> - Mobilize

In fact, many teachers and scholars are looking to *community organizing* as a model for teacher-leaders (Adler-Kassner; Adler-Kassner and O'Neill; Fleischer; Gallagher, "Educating"). According to these writers, teachers already have many of the skills and attitudes required of community organizers. Here, for example, is Cathy Fleischer:

> I think teachers are natural community organizers. Think what we do every day to create and sustain communities in our classrooms. We take a bunch of disparate individuals, sometimes up to 35 or 40 at a time, who bring diverse backgrounds, experiences, socioeconomic factors, race, gender, interest, reading level, skills, strengths, and motivations, and somehow—at our best—manage to form a cohesive group. (14–15)

Fleischer's book *Teachers Organizing for Change* provides compelling portraits of teachers organizing with parents to help shape educational practices and policies. Like the other writers we have cited here, Fleischer urges teachers to take a proactive, rather than reactive, stance. Again, this idea takes on special significance in light of the top-down, heavy-handed "reform" initiatives such as the Common Core State Standards Initiative that omit teachers from decision making.

There is, we recognize, a seeming contradiction here: we are calling on teachers to assert themselves and their professional judgment, to claim their unique expertise and grab the reins of educational reform, while we are promoting so-called soft skills such as adaptiveness, collaboration, and inquiry. But to our minds, this is not a contradiction once we accept this alternative way of thinking about leadership.[4] This is what Kathie came to recognize: that her leadership was not dependent on choosing between her own professional judgment and her commitment to collaboration and inquiry. Rather, her leadership became all the more potent through the combination of her own expertise and her ability to adapt and to collaborate with others. What is true of teachers is true of teacher-leaders as well: we are at our most effective when we are lead learners, not lead knowers. We need not have the loudest voices to have the deepest impact.

This is not to say that teacher-leaders should never raise their voices, make strong arguments, or be proactive and even aggressive. Teacher leadership comes in many forms, depending on who is practicing it and in what situations. Consider, for instance, the kind of leadership for writing assessment that former Michigan high school teacher Maja Wilson has practiced both locally and nationally.

Maja Raises Her Voice: Resisting Bad Assessment

> Yup, I've used rubrics. But let us call them what they are—cop-outs. I'd be insulted if I went to a writing workshop or an MFA class and got feedback based on a rubric. I'd demand my money back. I'd throw rotten tomatoes.[5]

So wrote Maja Wilson in the summer of 2004. At the time, Maja was a relatively new teacher, having taught both at traditional and alternative high schools for about five years. She was also a regular participant in a professional listserv, and this "rant," as she calls it, was an attempt to encourage her colleagues not to take rubrics for granted, but to explore alternative writing assessment options. (Because this story is not about rubrics per se, we don't reproduce Maja's specific charges against rubrics here, though they are referenced in Chapter 2. We encourage interested readers to read her *Rethinking Rubrics in Writing Assessment*.) The rant felt good, Maja says, and she was hoping it would make some people on the list think, but she didn't expect it to amount to much.

Then she received a note off-list from an editor at an educational press asking her if she would be interested in writing a book about rubrics. Once she was convinced the editor was serious, Maja jumped at the chance. Writing had long been her passion, and she'd wanted to write for publication for a long time, but she wasn't sure what she wanted to write about. Now she had her topic.

Maja scheduled a weekend writing retreat with a couple of teacher friends, and she set to work on the introduction to what would become her book, *Rethinking Rubrics in Writing Assessment*. At this retreat, one of her friends, a middle school teacher, began talking about an English language arts committee convened by their Intermediate School District (ISD), an organization that provides professional development and curriculum coordination across counties in Michigan. This committee was developing common curriculum and assessments across the counties for the elementary and middle school levels. Although her colleague was excited about this work, Maja says, "it did not sound like a good idea to me." In fact, it sounded like the kind of standardization of teaching and writing that she was arguing against in her book. When her friend informed her that the plan was to bring the work to the high school level, Maja knew she wanted to get on the committee. There was already a ninth-grade representative, but when Maja returned to school in the fall, she made the case to her principal that she should represent alternative education, and she got herself invited to join the committee.

After attending one or two meetings in the fall of 2004, Maja "pretty quickly realized that [her] leeriness was well-placed." The group mostly "moved state standards around on a chart" and then turned its attention to devising "suggested practices." Maja worried that these practices would be imposed on teachers. But her concerns were ratcheted up when the group began discussing assessment—which is to say, rubrics. Maja had done some research into the problems of using rubrics to teach and assess writing and was at that time reading Brian Huot's *(Re)Articulating Writing Assessment for Teaching and Learning*, which argues for local, context-sensitive writing assessment. So she began making the argument to the committee members that teachers should develop their own assessments rather than just use state or other rubrics. "That argument," Maja says, "wasn't received too well."

Undaunted, Maja continued to push back on the proposed rubrics and standardized assessments. That October, the ISD sponsored an inservice to which eighth-grade teachers were to bring their students' writing in response to common assessments. The idea was to conduct a scoring session in order to collect some initial data and to norm teachers' reading practices. There was no similar ninth-grade meeting, so Maja asked to sit in on the eighth-grade meeting. At this meeting, she says, "it was quite clear that a lot of the teachers were uncomfortable with the rubric." As they attempted to score student writing, Maja noticed they had trouble interpreting the performance descriptors, some of which provided two independent criteria (e.g., that ideas are "well developed" and "interesting"). Maja wanted to talk about the teachers' concerns, but the session leader did not listen for long. "Look," she said to Maja, "all of these teachers have spent a lot of time using this rubric, so we're not going to change it." She instructed Maja to stop talking about the rubric.

Maja got up and left, *(Re)Articulating Writing Assessment for Teaching and Learning* tucked under her arm. This was the first and only time Maja left a professional meeting in progress. She says this was a difficult decision for her, but, as she later said to the session leader when she returned to discuss the incident, it felt to her as if her perspective was not valued and the conversation was going nowhere. When she is resistant to what is happening in a professional context, Maja says, she works hard to push the conversation forward while remaining part of the group. "I think *constantly* about how to play that line," she says. In this instance, she felt that line was taken away from her, and her best option was to refuse further participation.

Soon after the meeting, Maja received a "talking to" from her principal, as word had gotten back to him about the meeting. Several weeks later, her principal told her that she should not go to the next committee meeting because he "needed [her] in the building." Maja determined that she could not change the committee "working from within," so she decided to enlist the support of her colleagues at the high school. She was sure they had no idea that the ISD committee planned to replace the curriculum that teachers had developed with the standardized one generated by the committee. "If no one's going to listen to me," she reasoned, "maybe they'll listen to the whole department." She met with the high school English language arts department chair and some of the ninth-grade teachers. They were receptive to her concerns and protective of the curriculum they had worked hard to develop. They called a meeting of the whole department, at which one colleague offered moving testimony about her previous experiences in a district with a tightly scripted curriculum and the heavy price she had paid for deviating from it. This meeting galvanized support for opting out of the ISD plans, and the high school teachers reached out to their middle school counterparts.

Next, the high school department head and Maja wrote a letter listing the accomplishments of the high school and middle school departments and arguing that "we don't need the ISD to tell us what to do." All the members of the high school and middle school departments signed the letter, and it was sent to the school administrators and the superintendent. A meeting of all the players was called.

The purpose of this meeting, Maja recalls, was "to tell the administrators how displeased we were and to request permission to pull out of the ISD curriculum and assessment scheme." A fellow high school teacher opened the meeting with an impassioned speech about academic freedom. He quoted Thoreau and promised to practice passive resistance if the committee had its way. At the end of this speech, everyone was silent and wide-eyed. Finally, a school administrator asked, "Does everyone feel like this?" The teachers nodded their heads in unison. "We thought everyone was on board with this," another administrator said. The teachers shook their heads no.

The high school principal granted the department permission to pull out of the ISD common curriculum and assessment scheme. (The middle school decided to keep its options open.) For Maja, this seemed an important step in avoiding the kinds of problems she was uncovering in her research on rubrics for the book. Indeed, her work with colleagues and her work on the book were "feeding each other," as she puts it. In particular, "the writing came to take on urgency because I saw the need for it." She had started writing the book mainly for herself: she wanted to better understand and be able to articulate her reservations about rubrics. But in light of the events going on in her school, the project had shifted from an explanation of why she didn't use rubrics to an argument "to maintain the choice not to use rubrics." Now "it was about creating a safe space where [she] didn't have to use rubrics." And it was about giving other teachers who shared her concerns a resource, a published book, that they could use to sharpen their own thinking or as support in conversations with their colleagues and administrators.

By the beginning of the 2005 school year, the book was drafted and submitted. Maja had played a role in fending off standardized curriculum and assessment in her school, and she wanted to turn her attention to "having an open conversation about assessment, to see what we could do together" in her school. Though Maja is not a proponent of assessment schemes in which every teacher is asked to take a single approach to assessment—"I'm just too leery of what is lost when everyone has to do the same thing, even if that 'same thing' is my idea"—she sees the value of teachers and students working together to assess writing.

But before she and her colleagues could get anything off the ground, they had another struggle on their hands: the ISD had shifted its focus from common curriculum and assessment to DuFour-model professional learning communities (PLCs), and teachers were being asked to focus their common plan time on "data." Maja suspected that this apparent shift in focus was really "another way to get at common assessments and common curriculum." Because the model being touted involved common assessments and the use of PLCs primarily to analyze data, it struck Maja as a kind of Trojan horse that would deliver the very assessments she and her colleagues had worked so hard to reject. She concluded that the teachers "had to fight this off or we'd be doing it to ourselves." So she asked to be put on the school improvement committee.

Here her arguments found traction, and the committee was soon discussing the need to talk about teaching *before* looking at student work. "If you haven't talked about teaching and learning and different frames for approaching the work, you're not necessarily changing anything if you look at student work," Maja argued. "'Data' do not improve schools; only better teaching will give students a better experience at school."

> **"Data" do not improve schools; only better teaching will give students a better experience at school.**
>
> **—Maja Wilson**

Eventually, the school improvement committee offered to do all the professional development for the school "inhouse," again opting out of the ISD scheme. This was not an easy argument to make—especially the part about talking about teaching before looking at student work, since there is so much pressure on schools, and particularly administrators, to provide "data." Maja says her administrator needed to hear the arguments repeatedly, but he finally agreed and became a staunch defender of the school improvement committee, whose alternative approach to PLCs was featured in a presentation at the 2010 NCTE Annual Convention. The school improvement committee continues today to provide professional development for the teachers at the high school and, as Maja puts it, "continues to insist on the danger of a single-minded focus on data collection."

Maja left her position at the high school in 2008 to pursue graduate study, so she has not participated in the development of alternative local assessments. But her story is less about designing "good assessment" than clearing a space for it by resisting "bad assessment." Perhaps unfortunately, this too is part of a teacher-leader's job in the current education environment.

According to Maja, writing *Rethinking Rubrics in Writing Assessment* "emboldened me in the sense that I felt really, really clear about what I thought and knew and really, really clear about how PLCs would get in the way." Not all teachers would reach the same conclusions Maja reached, of course, and not all of us will write books about our beliefs about teaching and assessing writing. Maja is exceptional in having provided leadership for change both locally and, through her book and her presentations, nationally. Still, her practice of leadership bears the hallmarks of the approach we outline in this chapter. It is rooted in inquiry into her ideas and beliefs about teaching, learning, writing, and assessment. (After all, she researched and wrote a book about teaching and assessing writing while she was a practicing teacher.) It is collaborative, placing a premium on organizing and mobilizing others. And it is adaptive, responding to changing circumstances.

Teachers practice leadership in different ways, as Kathie and Maja show, but effective teacher leadership is always adaptive. Teacher-leaders must be attuned to the situations in which they find themselves, constantly looking for—and, when necessary, as we've seen with Maja, *creating*—opportunities to shape policy and practice. This has been a hallmark of the career of our final featured teacher, Laura Roop, a former high school teacher and current codirector of the Oakland (Michigan) Writing Project and director of outreach at the University of Michigan School of Education.[6]

Laura Looks for Openings: Finding and Creating Moments of Opportunity

Like Kathie, when Laura began her career as a high school teacher—in the mid-1980s, after serving a few years as a writing specialist at the University of Michigan's Reading and Writing Skills Center—she did not have a particular interest in leadership or in policy; she was focused on providing the best instruction for her students. To that end, the summer after her first year of classroom teaching, she attended the Oakland Writing Project (OWP) Invitational Summer Institute. The next fall, at the urging of the OWP director, she began offering professional development sessions on teaching poetry for her teacher peers in the county. Four years later, Laura became director of the OWP and a literacy consultant working with twenty-eight school districts. In this role, she says, she "began to understand the tremendous inequities that existed between classrooms, schools, and districts." Spurred in part by this recognition, she took a position as a networking specialist with the Michigan Partnership for New Education, a state reform effort housed at Michigan State University. When this initiative morphed in ways that made Laura uncomfortable, she was hired as dissemination coordinator, professional development facilitator, and middle school task force leader for the Michigan English Language Arts Framework (MELAF) project, a federally funded state standards effort. After five years of this work, she completed her dissertation, was hired into her current position as director of outreach for the University of Michigan, and resumed her role as director of the OWP.

As this brief bio suggests, Laura has had a long and complicated relationship with educational "reform." While she has always thought of herself first and foremost as a teacher, increasingly she has been drawn to work that allows her to expand her sphere of influence among her peers as well as policymakers. This has placed her in the middle of significant reform efforts and engaged her in policy work. Her involvement with policy, Laura says, has become important to her because "policy affects what is possible in classrooms." She speaks of "nested contexts": classrooms within schools, schools within districts, districts within states, states within the nation, the nation within the world. Because each context shapes the next, Laura says, "as a teacher, you can't just shut the classroom door."

> **Policy affects what is possible in classrooms. . . . As a teacher, you can't just shut the classroom door.**
>
> **–Laura Roop**

Laura learned this lesson early on in her career when an enterprising legislator added to Michigan law a requirement that high school students complete portfolios to showcase their work. Knowledgeable about the power of writing portfolios, which at the time were gaining many adherents among writing teachers and researchers (see, for instance, Belanoff and Dickson; Black, Daiker, Sommers, and Stygall; Graves and Sunstein), Laura was initially intrigued by the possibilities of these portfolios to support student learning. However, she quickly came to see that employability skills portfolios (ESPs), included as a requirement in the State School Aid Act in 1991, were an example of "a good idea turned into a bad practice." First, as the name suggests, the ESPs were narrowly confined to career preparation. Second, as Laura recalls, "schools rushed to minimal compliance," treating the portfolios as an accountability device only, rather than as a learning tool for their students. As a result, school personnel began filling large file cabinets with folders, but teaching and learning were unaffected.

Still, Laura and her Writing Project colleagues saw an opportunity. In practice, the ESPs were proving to be a perversion of what Laura and her colleagues knew was most important about portfolios: their ability to capture student learning and performance in complex ways by sponsoring reflection, collecting work over time, displaying work in multiple genres for various purposes and audiences, and so on. But the fact that legislators wanted a portfolio in the first place—for whatever reason, and even if they didn't know why—created an opening to push for, in Laura's words, "something much more interesting" than pen-and-paper standardized tests.

And they had an idea about how to do that. They arranged some meetings with University of Michigan colleagues who had begun work on required writing portfolios for incoming students. They knew the university's approach to portfolios would have a profound influence on how districts approached this work, so they endeavored to leverage collaboration between the University of Michigan faculty and their teaching networks to develop a more robust vision for student writing portfolios. As it turned out, the ESPs were dropped from the State School Aid requirements in the mid-1990s and the state implemented an essay-based writing proficiency test, but the partnership Laura and her OWP colleagues forged with their University of Michigan colleagues keeps portfolios on the state's collective radar and in districts' practice.

For Laura, the initial implementation of ESPs and the proficiency tests, while not themselves positive developments, created moments of opportunity. While she's seen many good ideas turn into bad practices, she asks herself "How can we legitimate the good student work that people want, even if those people keep doing the wrong things to support that work?"

Laura's work with OWP colleagues on developing professional development around the Michigan English Language Arts Framework in the 1990s provides an apt example. As she and her colleagues suggest in a National Writing Project monograph, standards can be viewed as a tool for reflection, but "when standards projects reify curriculum, freezing educators into lockstep form, and when such projects collapse the complexities of assessment into the single lens of standardized tests, they cease serving teachers, students, and democratic societies" (Koch, Roop, and Setter 1). The OWP worked with schools to develop teacher inquiry and leadership in the context of standards and benchmarks through action research, collaboration, and professional sharing (including publishing). According to Laura and her colleagues, the principal achievements of their professional development program were these:

- the development of individual teacher knowledge and leadership regarding standards
- the design and piloting of multidistrict, standards-based, high-quality professional development
- the establishment of new norms for cross-district and cross-level learning
- the creation of a support network for districts and schools attempting to enact standards and benchmarks (10)

While the OWP leaders clearly recognized the perils of standards, they saw in the MELAF project an opportunity to develop teacher leadership and spur positive change.

Recently, Laura and her Writing Project colleagues identified another moment of opportunity. In the wake of the current economic downturn, Michigan is attempting to make its assessment system leaner by cutting assessments. At the same time, like many states it is looking to Internet-enabled technologies to support cost cutting. Laura and her colleagues understand that the state has to do *something* but does not want to send the message that it does not value writing. So they see another opportunity to assert the value of portfolios.

Indeed, Laura imagines "a portfolio revival for the digital age." She wants to harness the energy of emerging electronic portfolio research and practice—including in the new high-tech high schools and International Baccalaureate schools in her state—to push for the piloting of electronic portfolio assessment in Michigan high schools. (See the extensive—and growing—bibliography on e-portfolio research on the Inter/National Coalition for Electronic Portfolio Research website: http://ncepr.org/bibliography.html.) Laura and her colleagues are meeting with assessment and curriculum and instruction staff at the Michigan Department of Education as well as the University of Michigan to explore the idea that e-portfolios could support student learning as they make the transition from high school into college and the workforce.

It is too early to say what will come of these meetings, but Laura is hopeful that this good idea can be turned into good practice. "Now is the time," she says, "to fight for the kinds of literacies and the kinds of assessment we've been saying we want for the past twenty years."

Now Is the Time

These are indeed dark days for teachers. Today's schools do not meet Dewey's simple but powerful criterion for the honorific "democratic": they are not "organized in such a way that every teacher has some regular and representative way in which he or she can register judgment upon matters of educational importance, with the assurance that this judgment will somehow affect the school system" ("Democracy" 195). Indeed, teachers are systematically disenfranchised. The current economic crisis is only worsening this state of affairs as teachers fear dire repercussions for speaking out. This does not bode well for education, both because those who know the most about teaching and learning are removed from decision making and because we know that controlled teachers—those who manage to stick it out in a profession with fewer and fewer rewards and more and more constraints—are more likely to become controlling teachers (McNeil; Wasley).

At the same time, we have chosen to end this chapter with Laura's clarion call because we share her hope and her conviction that the time is right to advocate for the kinds of literacies and assessments we value. Teachers have led through dark days and into brave new worlds before, and we must do so again—humbly, as inquirers and collaborators, and assertively, knowing that our teaching and our students' learning rests, as it should and must, on our better judgment.

Notes

1. In making this argument, we diverge from the SARW Standard 10, which holds that "[a]ll stakeholders in the educational community—students, families, teachers, administrators, policymakers, and the public—must have an equal voice in the development, interpretation, and reporting of assessment information" (28). While we do not have space to develop this argument at length here, we believe the voices of teachers and students ought to be privileged in educational assessment, as they are the primary actors in teaching and learning activities in schools. See Gallagher's "Being There" for a critique of the "stakeholder theory of power" and an alternative approach that privileges students and teachers in educational decision making.

2. To protect the privacy of our interlocutors, these exchanges are based closely on actual correspondences but are not verbatim reproductions.

3. As one of our respondents at the beginning of this chapter mentions, however, the federal government eliminated direct funding for the National Writing Project in 2011. The NWP continues to compete for Department of Education funding and to seek alternative sources of funding. For the latest news and information on ways to help the cause, see nwpworks.ning.com.

4. Our notion of leadership is informed as well by feminist theories, which also tend to emphasize leadership as an activity rather than a condition or a role. In feminist perspectives, leadership is typically rendered as relational, self-reflective, inclusive, community-

minded, and shared or distributed. On feminism, women, and educational leadership, see Blackmore; Reynolds; and Strachan.

Though we don't have space to pursue this here, it is also worth noting the gendered nature of the concepts of "expertise" and "leadership." Writers such as Linda Darling-Hammond, Margaret Marshall, and David Tyack have explored the historical connections between hierarchical school systems and constructions of female teachers as obedient and compliant. The derogation of teachers discussed early in this chapter is surely influenced by cultural constructions of "women's work."

We are also mindful that most of the examples in this book, which is coauthored by two men, feature women. While we did attempt, unsuccessfully, to cultivate more examples that featured men, we did not strive for perfect gender balance, and we are glad we are able to feature the wonderful work of so many women; perhaps in some small way, this pushes back against the derogation of "women's work." In any case, we have worked closely with each featured teacher throughout the development of the examples, often essentially co-drafting them. In the process, we have worked hard to tell the story that the teachers wish to have told and to leave plenty of room for their voices, when that was what they desired. In each case, they had the final say in what was included in the example and how it was presented. We recognize, however, our own limitations, as men, in this area, as well as the limitations (and affordances) of the approach we've taken. We hope to write about these issues in a subsequent project.

5. We reproduce here what Maja reports to have written; this is not a transcript from a listserv archive, which we were unable to locate.

6. When we shared a draft of this chapter with Laura, she insisted that the story we tell in her example "is a collective story. . . . I am not the only one involved!" She then cited several colleagues who played pivotal roles in supporting meaningful teaching and writing in Michigan over the past couple of decades, including her husband, Richard Koch; his colleagues in Lenawee County, Michigan; Jay Robinson at the University of Michigan; Ellen Brinkley at Western Michigan University; Mary Cox at the Meadowbrook Writing Project; and many others who have played instrumental roles in helping support meaningful teaching and learning of writing in Michigan. We are happy to share this acknowledgment.

Our Best Hope

Epilogue

We often ask our students, "What is your best hope for your writing?" It is an important question, we think, because writers do their best work when they believe that their writing matters—that it can have a significant impact on those who read it. So what is our best hope for *Our Better Judgment*? What do we hope happens when a reader finishes this epilogue and puts down the book?

First, you—as we'll call this reader—are *ready to take action*. You are convinced that the stakes are too high for teachers to step aside while noneducators dictate what happens in classrooms and schools. You are not naïve about the political, economic, and social forces that shape teachers' and students' work together, but you believe meaningful, effective educational experiences cannot be run by remote control; rather, they can emerge only from inside classrooms and schools. And you believe assessment is critical to this work both because it is a means of control wielded by "reformers" for political ends *and* because it is a means of inquiry wielded by teachers for educational ends. Because you believe "the teacher is the most important agent of assessment" (Standard 2, SARW), you are prepared to use assessment to "speak back" to those "reformers."

Because you believe "the primary purpose of assessment is to improve teaching and learning" (Standard 3, SARW), you are prepared to use assessment to help your students write in ways that matter to them and in their worlds. And because you believe writing is a key means by which people of all walks of life learn and communicate in the twenty-first century, you are eager to use writing assessment to help your students do just that.

Second, you *know what to do*—or at least how to get started and how to learn more. You know what writing assessment looks like in an inquiry framework, and you know how to take next steps from wherever you are. You understand that the context in which you teach is unique, and you know how to use writing assessment as inquiry into how students write and learn in your classroom and school. You know teachers are uniquely positioned to conduct writing assessment, and you know how to work with your students and your colleagues to ask good questions, collect good information, and use what you learn to support teaching and learning. You might start by:

> • Reflecting on how and when you use rubrics in your classroom. Who writes the rubrics that you use? How do you understand what is being valued on the rubric? How do your students understand these tools? Do you always need a rubric to assess students' writing? Are there other tools that might help you arrive at judgments about your students' writing? Maybe this reflection will lead you to revise your approach to rubrics and responding to and assessing student writing.

> • Sponsoring a conversation (or a series of conversations) with your students about what they think is important in their writing, inviting them to articulate their values and construct and participate in assessing their own and their peers' writing. Maybe this will provide you with new insight on how to value and assess writing in your classroom.

> • Creating a sequence of formative writing assessments in your classroom, allowing you to trace a component of student writing that you are curious about or with which you have seen students struggle again and again. Maybe these smaller, formative assessments will help you revise instructional practices and make your values clearer to your students.

> • Using Web-based technologies that allow students to compose and assess their writing and to converse with and be assessed by people within and beyond the walls of the classroom. Maybe this will help you and your students imagine new ways of assessing and composing or discover the nuances of composing in a digital media rather than with pen and paper.

> • Reading an article or book, maybe one listed in the appendix or the annotated bibliography, to help you discover something new about writing assessment. Maybe this new knowledge will cycle back into your

classroom by giving you a new approach to assessment, a new method for teaching, or simply a better, more interesting question about your students' writing and learning.

In addition to knowing how to pursue assessment-as-inquiry in your classroom with your students, you also know how to seek inquiry-based conversation and collaboration with colleagues and community members, including parents. You might consider:

  • Making the discussion of writing assessment a priority within your professional learning community or department. You could encourage teachers to bring in samples of student work to meetings and use the students' texts as the foundation for a conversation on strengths and weaknesses of writing instruction within the department. Or you could work as a staff to unpack the state rubric used on your students' writing and to put those values in conversation with the values of your district, school, and program—as well as your own values. Or you could experiment with alternative forms of assessment such as yearlong or careerlong portfolios. Regardless of how you engage your colleagues, you could promote the discussion of writing and writing assessment by inquiring into student writing and instructional practice. Maybe these activities will help shape a new culture of writing and writing assessment in your school.

  • Inviting community members, including parents, into the assessment process by "borrowing" their experience or inviting them to mentor students in new genres and discourses. Community members might serve as conversation partners with both students and teachers and perhaps as assessors of their writing. Maybe these collaborations will help connect the school more closely to the community while helping prepare students for life after they leave school.

  • Researching and writing about writing assessment in your classroom and school. You might become active as a teacher-researcher, sharing your discoveries with other teachers by presenting and publishing your research and assessment practices at conferences, online teaching websites, and journals. Maybe this work will make public your expertise and allow you to shape writing assessment conversations within and beyond your school and district.

  • Organizing local or grassroots teacher activist groups that help inform various constituents about what is occurring at the state or federal level with writing and literacy assessment practices. Or you could work to get yourself or other teachers on committees—district, state level, professional—that create assessments or have an influence on shaping policy in order to present teachers' perspectives in the conversation. Maybe you and your colleagues will help shape the next generation of writing assessments.

No matter what your next step is, we hope you are inspired to undertake it in the spirit of inquiry and for the sake of your students' learning and your own.

Finally, you *are emboldened* to take the writing assessment reins and help your colleagues and students succeed in this brave new world of writing and writing assessment. You are aware that policymakers, outside "experts," and "educational services" companies promote assessment as a technical utopia of objective measurement, and you understand the potential dystopian effect this approach could have on schooling. You know that education is more meaningful and powerful when teachers and students are understood as sources, rather than recipients, of expertise and judgment. You understand that writing assessment is neither magic nor a precise technical science. You understand that, like your students, you must start from where you are, doing what you can, and go from there. From the examples in this book, you understand that teachers like you *can* develop writing assessment literacy, expertise, and leadership. You will learn what you need to know to make writing assessment meaningful and effective in your classroom (see the appendix and annotated bibliography). You will work with your colleagues and partners outside your classroom and school to develop, expand, and deepen your writing assessment expertise. You will practice leadership by helping organize and mobilize others to support students as writers and learners. You will do all this because you know you *should* and you know you *can*. You will do it because you know your judgment, honed by inquiry and experience, matters. You will do it because your students deserve no less. You will do it because you are a teacher.

Appendix

Selected Assessment Resources

General Assessment

Andrade, Heidi L., and Gregory J. Cizek, eds. *Handbook of Formative Assessment*. New York: Routledge, 2009. Print.

Black, Paul, Christine Harrison, Clare Lee, Bethan Marshall, and Dylan Wiliam. *Assessment for Learning: Putting It into Practice*. Maidenhead, UK: Open Univ. Press, 2003. Print.

———. "Working Inside the Black Box: Assessment for Learning in the Classroom." *Phi Delta Kappan* 86.1 (2004): 8–21. Print.

Black, Paul, and Dylan Wiliam. "Inside the Black Box: Raising Standards through Classroom Assessment." *Phi Delta Kappan* 80.2 (1998): 139–48. Print.

Butler, Susan M., and Nancy D. McMunn. *A Teacher's Guide to Classroom Assessment: Understanding and Using Assessment to Improve Student Learning*. San Francisco: Jossey-Bass, 2006. Print.

Fairtest.org. The National Center for Fair and Open Testing. Web.

Gallagher, Chris W. *Reclaiming Assessment: A Better Alternative to the Accountability Agenda*. Portsmouth, NH: Heinemann, 2007. Print.

Guskey, Thomas R. "How Classroom Assessments Improve Learning." *Educational Leadership* 60.5 (2003): 6–11. Print.

Lukin, Leslie E., Deborah L. Bandalos, Teresa J. Eckhout, and Kristine Mickelson. "Facilitating the Development of Assessment Literacy." *Educational Measurement: Issues and Practice* 23.2 (2004): 26–32. Print.

Popham, W. James. *Classroom Assessment: What Teachers Need to Know*. 6th ed. Upper Saddle River, NJ: Prentice, 2010. Print.

———. *The Truth about Testing: An Educator's Call to Action*. Washington, DC: Association for Supervision and Curriculum Development, 2001. Print.

Stephens, Diane, and Jennifer Strong, eds. *Assessment as Inquiry: Learning the Hypothesis-Test Process*. Urbana, IL: NCTE, 1999. Print.

Stiggins, Rick J., and Jan Chappuis. *An Introduction to Student-Involved Assessment FOR Learning*. 6th ed. Boston: Pearson, 2012. Print.

Wiggins, Grant. *Educative Assessment: Designing Assessment to Inform and Improve Student Performance*. San Francisco: Jossey-Bass, 1998. Print.

Literacy Assessment

Dolgin, Joanna, Kim Kelly, and Sarvenaz Zelkha. *Authentic Assessments for the English Classroom*. Urbana, IL: NCTE, 2010. Print.

Johnston, Peter H. *Constructive Evaluation of Literate Activity*. New York: Longman, 1992. Print.

———. *Knowing Literacy: Constructive Literacy Assessment*. Portland, ME: Stenhouse, 1997. Print.

National Council of Teachers of English. "NCTE Position Statements on Assessment and Testing." NCTE, n.d. Web. 13 June 2011.

Writing Assessment

Adler-Kassner, Linda, and Peggy O'Neill. *Reframing Writing Assessment to Improve Teaching and Learning*. Logan: Utah State UP, 2010. Print.

Anderson, Susan Lee. "The Instructional Practices of Teachers Who Score a State Writing Assessment: A Case Study." Diss. U of Nebraska-Lincoln, 2009. *UNL DigitalCommons*. Web. 20 Aug. 2010.

Assessing Writing (journal).

Broad, Bob. *What We Really Value: Beyond Rubrics in Teaching and Assessing Writing*. Logan: Utah State UP, 2003. Print.

Broad, Bob, Linda Adler-Kassner, Barry Alford, Jane Detweiler, Heidi Estrem, Susanmarie Harrington, Maureen McBride, Eric Stalions, and Scott Weedon. *Organic Writing Assessment: Dynamic Criteria Mapping in Action*. Logan: Utah State UP, 2009. Print.

CCCC Committee on Assessment. "Writing Assessment: A Position Statement." *College Composition and Communication* 46.3 (1995): 430–37. Print.

Dappen, Leon, Jody Isernhagen, and Sue Anderson. "A Statewide Writing Assessment Model: Student Proficiency and Future Implications." *Assessing Writing* 13.1 (2008): 45-60. Print.

Elliot, Norbert. *On a Scale: A Social History of Writing Assessment in America*. New York: Lang, 2005. Print.

Haswell, Richard H., ed. *Beyond Outcomes: Assessment and Instruction within a University Writing Program*. Westport, CT: Ablex, 2001. Print.

Herrington, Anne, Kevin Hodgson, and Charles Moran, eds. *Teaching the New Writing: Technology, Change, and Assessment in the 21st-Century Classroom*. New York: Teachers College; Berkeley, CA: National Writing Project, 2009. Print.

Hillocks, George, Jr. *The Testing Trap: How State Writing Assessments Control Learning*. New York: Teachers College, 2002. Print.

Huot, Brian. *(Re)Articulating Writing Assessment for Teaching and Learning*. Logan: Utah State UP, 2002. Print.

Huot, Brian, and Peggy O'Neil, eds. *Assessing Writing: A Critical Sourcebook*. Boston: Bedford/St. Martin's; Urbana, IL: NCTE, 2008. Print.

Journal of Writing Assessment. Print.

Turley, Eric D. "The Scientific Management of Writing and the Residue of Reform." Diss. U of Nebraska-Lincoln, 2008. *UNL DigitalCommons*. Web. 20 Aug. 2010.

Turley, Eric D., and Chris W. Gallagher. "On the *Uses* of Rubrics: Reframing the Great Rubric Debate." *English Journal* 97.4 (2008): 87–92. Print.

White, Edward M., William D. Lutz, and Sandra Kamusikiri, eds. *Assessment of Writing: Politics, Policies, Practices*. New York: MLA, 1996. Print.

Wilson, Maja. *Rethinking Rubrics in Writing Assessment*. Portsmouth, NH: Heinemann, 2006. Print.

Annotated Bibliography

Andrade, Heidi L., and Gregory J. Cizek, eds.
Handbook of Formative Assessment
New York: Routledge, 2009. Print.

This book is a comprehensive and readable primer on theory, practice, and policy issues related to formative assessment. It includes twenty chapters, written by leading formative assessment researchers and scholars, covering classroom and large-scale formative assessment in K–12 and postsecondary contexts. The book is aimed at teachers, researchers, and policymakers, and most of the chapters are accessible to all of these audiences. It is also forward-looking: the last section explores "challenges and future directions for formative assessment."

Assessing Writing (journal)
Print.

Founded in 1994, this is the first journal devoted entirely to writing assessment. International in scope, *AW* publishes articles, book reviews, and other occasional pieces on a wide range of topics related to writing assessment, both classroom and large scale, K–12 and college/university, formative and summative, school based and community based. Its audience consists of teachers, researchers, and writing assessment experts around the world, though articles are published only in English.

Broad, Bob
What We Really Value: Beyond Rubrics in Teaching and Assessing Writing
Logan: Utah State UP, 2003. Print.

Written primarily for postsecondary writing teachers and administrators, this book is nonetheless useful for K–12 teachers in its demonstration of a process that teachers can undertake to reveal and document "what they really value" in student writing. Broad provides a history and critique of traditional rubrics and offers as an alternative a process he calls "dynamic criteria mapping" (DCM). The purpose of DCM is to capture and represent the values of a writing program in a more complex and useful way than reductive rubrics can. Broad offers a detailed case study of teachers in the first-year composition program at "City University" developing their maps through conversation and negotiation. His follow-up, coauthored book *Organic Writing Assessment* provides several more DCM case studies at a range of institutions.

Fairtest.org.
Web.

This website is hosted by the National Center for Fair and Open Testing (FairTest), an organization that "advances quality education and equal opportunity by promoting fair, open, valid and educationally beneficial evaluations of students, teachers and schools. FairTest also works to end the misuses and flaws of testing practices that impede these goals." A virtual clearinghouse for resources on K–12 and postsecondary assessment, the site houses a newsletter, research reports, fact sheets, informational videos, media kits, organizing tools, links to other helpful websites, and a network of educators and activists devoted to FairTest's principles. It will be useful to anyone looking for information about the effects of standardized testing on teaching and learning and/or hoping to become involved in the struggle for fair and open assessment practices.

Gallagher, Chris W.
Reclaiming Assessment: A Better Alternative to the Accountability Agenda.
Portsmouth, NH: Heinemann, 2007. Print.

Based on a case study of Nebraska's rejection of high-stakes standardized tests in favor of a locally controlled, school-based, teacher-led system, this book shows what it looks like when teachers and students, rather than standardized tests, are put at the center of educational assessment. With chapters devoted to "making assessment meaningful in the classroom," "creating new models of professional development," and "extending the conversation into the community," Gallagher emphasizes the importance of building strong relationships inside and beyond schools. This book is written for teachers and includes a variety of practical examples of teachers working with students, one another, and parents and community members to conduct meaningful assessments that meet technical quality expectations.

Huot, Brian
(Re)Articulating Writing Assessment for Teaching and Learning
Logan: Utah State UP, 2002. Print.

This book is written primarily for a postsecondary audience, but K–12 teachers will find it valuable for its positive, proactive approach to writing assessment. Drawing on writing assessment history and theory, Huot argues that writing assessment has been used as a means of social control by powerful interests, but that its roots lie in the teaching and learning relationship. Huot wants teachers to reconnect to writing assessment rather than being scared off by technical jargon. In his new version of writing assessment, writing studies and educational measurement specialists will work together across disciplines to develop new models of validity and reliability, and teachers—rather than administrators and testers—will control educational assessment.

Johnston, Peter H.
Knowing Literacy: Constructive Literacy Assessment
Portland, ME: Stenhouse, 1997. Print.

Written by the chair of the IRA–NCTE Joint Task Force on Assessment, which created the _Standards for the Assessment of Reading and Writing_, this book reminds us that assessment is not only a "technical problem," but also and primarily a

human one. Johnston argues that effective literacy assessment must be informed by a working knowledge of children's literacy and learning. The book therefore explores assessment and literacy side by side, as social and educational practices that teachers and students engage in together. Johnston places heavy emphasis on tracking and documenting student learning, especially using portfolios, running records, and observation sheets. The book also guides readers in talking with others in school communities about literacy, learning, and assessment.

Journal of Writing Assessment
Print.

Founded in 2003, this journal publishes articles, book reviews, and annotated bibliographies from many disciplines on a wide variety of topics, including the history and theory of writing assessment, assessment policies, program assessment, and grading and response. It covers writing assessment in schools (K–12 and postsecondary) and in nonschool settings.

National Council of Teachers of English
"NCTE Position Statements on Assessment and Testing"
NCTE, n.d. Web. 13 June 2011.

This website gathers together more than thirty of NCTE's statements, guidelines, and resolutions dating back to 1970. The IRA–NCTE _Standards for the Assessment of Reading and Writing_ is of course included, as are other key professional statements such as the _NCTE Framework for 21st Century Curriculum and Assessment_ (2008), _The Impact of the SAT and ACT Timed Writing Tests_ (2005), _Framing Statements on Assessment_ (2004), the _Resolution on Urging Reconsideration of High Stakes Testing_ (2000), and an array of statements related to postsecondary writing assessment. Together, these documents represent "the state of the art" of reading and writing assessment according to the national professional organization devoted to teaching English.

Popham, W. James
Classroom Assessment: What Teachers Need to Know
6th ed. Upper Saddle River, NJ: Prentice, 2010. Print.

In a friendly and often humorous tone, Popham, a leading proponent of high-quality formative and classroom assessments, offers a useful guide to classroom assessment for teachers. This book is designed as a textbook aimed primarily at new teachers in preservice courses. It introduces traditional measurement concepts such as validity and reliability in Popham's trademark accessible style. It also provides many practical examples of classroom strategies, some helpful exercises for teachers, scenarios to think with ("Extended Applications"), and an overview of research on classroom assessment.

Stiggins, Rick J., and Jan Chappuis
An Introduction to Student-Involved Assessment FOR Learning
6th ed. Boston: Pearson, 2012. Print.

This book, cowritten by the founder of the Assessment Training Institute (for a time part of ETS and recently purchased by Pearson), demonstrates how teachers can develop assessments that engage students and motivate them to learn while accurately reflecting their abilities. Often used in preservice and graduate-level education courses, the book is full of practical examples and hands-on exercises. Stiggins and Chappuis cover a range of assessment methods—including selected response, essays, performances, record keeping, conferences, and portfolios—with a focus on assessment purposes. Throughout, as the title of the book suggests, the authors emphasize the involvement of students in assessing their own learning.

Wilson, Maja
Rethinking Rubrics in Writing Assessment
Portsmouth, NH: Heinemann, 2006. Print.

In this book, Wilson, a high school teacher, explores the history and practice of rubrics in writing assessment, concluding that they limit and distort teaching and learning by standardizing and reductively quantifying response. Writing from her own classroom experiences, Wilson offers an accessible and controversial treatment of rubrics and outlines "a new writing assessment paradigm" that highlights readers' disagreement and human subjectivity. She concludes the book with a useful discussion of how teachers can find time to assess writing without rubrics.

Works Cited

Adler-Kassner, Linda. *The Activist WPA*. Logan: Utah State UP, 2008. Print.

Adler-Kassner, Linda, and Peggy O'Neill. *Reframing Writing Assessment to Improve Teaching and Learning*. Logan: Utah State UP, 2010. Print.

Andrade, Heidi L. "Students as the Definitive Source of Formative Assessment: Academic Self-Assessment and the Self-Regulation of Learning." Andrade and Cizek 90–105.

Andrade, Heidi L., and Gregory J. Cizek, eds. *Handbook of Formative Assessment*. New York: Routledge, 2009. Print.

Aristotle. *Nicomachean Ethics*. Trans. W. D. Ross. The Internet Classics Archive, n.d. Web. 13 June 2011.

Atwell, Nancie. *In the Middle: New Understandings about Writing, Reading, and Learning*. Portsmouth, NH: Boynton/Cook, 1998. Print.

Barth, Roland S. *Learning by Heart*. San Francisco: Jossey-Bass, 2001. Print.

Beers, Kylene. "An Open Letter to NCTE Members about the Release of the September Public Draft of the Common Core State Standards." NCTE, 21 Sept. 2009. Web. 3 May 2011.

Beers, Kylene, Robert E. Probst, and Linda Rief, eds. *Adolescent Literacy: Turning Promise into Practice*. Portsmouth, NH: Heinemann, 2007. Print.

Belanoff, Pat, and Marcia Dickson. *Portfolios: Process and Product*. Portsmouth, NH: Boynton/Cook, 1991. Print.

Berliner, David C., and Bruce J. Biddle. *The Manufactured Crisis: Myths, Fraud, and the Attack on America's Public Schools*. New York: Perseus, 1995. Print.

Black, Laurel, Donald A. Daiker, Jeffrey Sommers, and Gail Stygall, eds. *New Directions in Portfolio Assessment: Reflective Practice, Critical Theory, and Large-Scale Scoring*. Portsmouth, NH: Boynton/Cook, 1994. Print.

Black, Paul, Christine Harrison, Clare Lee, Bethan Marshall, and Dylan Wiliam. *Assessment for Learning: Putting It into Practice*. Maidenhead, UK: Open Univ. Press, 2003. Print.

———. "Working Inside the Black Box: Assessment for Learning in the Classroom." *Phi Delta Kappan* 86.1 (2004): 8–21. Print.

Black, Paul, and Dylan Wiliam. "Inside the Black Box: Raising Standards through Classroom Assessment." *Phi Delta Kappan* 80.2 (1998): 139–48. Print.

Blackmore, Jill. *Troubling Women: Feminism, Leadership and Educational Change*. Philadelphia: Open Univ. Press, 1999. Print.

Broad, Bob. *What We Really Value: Beyond Rubrics in Teaching and Assessing Writing*. Logan: Utah State UP, 2003. Print.

Cassell, Eric J. *Doctoring: The Nature of Primary Care Medicine*. New York: Oxford UP, 1997. Print.

Center for Media Literacy. "Literacy for the 21st Century: The Hope and the Promise." CML, n.d. Web. 3 May 2011.

Cochran-Smith, Marilyn, and Susan L. Lytle. *Inquiry as Stance: Practitioner Research for the Next Generation*. New York: Teachers College, 2009. Print.

———. *Inside/Outside: Teacher Research and Knowledge*. New York: Teachers College, 1993. Print.

Common Core State Standards Initiative. "Mission Statement." CCSSI, 2011. Web. 11 July 2011.

Comstock, Michelle, Mary Ann Cain, and Lil Brannon. *Composing Public Space: Teaching Writing in the Face of Private Interests*. Portsmouth, NH: Boynton/Cook, 2010. Print.

Darling-Hammond, Linda. *The Right to Learn: A Blueprint for Creating Schools that Work*. San Francisco: Jossey-Bass, 1997. Print.

Darling-Hammond, Linda, and Gary Sykes. *Teaching as the Learning Profession: Handbook of Policy and Practice*. San Francisco: Jossey-Bass, 1999. Print.

Deal, Terrence E., and Kent D. Peterson. *Shaping School Culture: The Heart of Leadership*. San Francisco: Jossey-Bass, 1999. Print.

Dewey, John. "Democracy in Education." *Elementary School Teacher* 4.4 (1903): 193–204. Print.

———. "Progressive Education and the Science of Education." 1928. *John Dewey on Education: Selected Writings*. Ed. Reginald D. Archambault. Chicago: U of Chicago P, 1974. 169–81. Print.

DuFour, Richard. "What Is a 'Professional Learning Community?'" *Educational Leadership* 61.8 (2004): 6–11. Print.

DuFour, Richard, and Robert Eaker. *Professional Learning Communities at Work: Best Practices for Enhancing Student Achievement*. Bloomington, IN: Solution Tree; Alexandria, VA: ASCD, 1998. Print.

Educators and Parents Against Testing Abuse. "EPATA Goals." Blog. *Testingabuse*. EPATA, 20 Feb. 2005. Web. 8 July 2011. <http://testingabuse.blogspot.com/2005_02_01_archive.html>.

Elliot, Norbert. *On a Scale: A Social History of Writing Assessment in America*. New York: Lang, 2005. Print.

Elmore, Richard F. *School Reform from the Inside Out: Policy, Practice, and Performance*. Cambridge, MA: Harvard Education P, 2004. Print.

Fairtest.org. The National Center for Fair and Open Testing. Web.

Fleischer, Cathy. *Teachers Organizing for Change: Making Literacy Learning Everybody's Business*. Urbana, IL: NCTE, 2000. Print.

Fullan, Michael. *Change Forces: Probing the Depths of Educational Reform*. New York: Falmer, 1993. Print.

Gallagher, Chris W. "Being There: (Re)Making the Assessment Scene." *College Composition and Communication* 62.3 (2011): 450–76. Print.

———. "Educating and Organizing for the Long Haul." *Constructivist Teacher* 19.1 (2008). Web. 13 June 2011.

———. *Reclaiming Assessment: A Better Alternative to the Accountability Agenda*. Portsmouth, NH: Heinemann, 2007. Print.

Gallagher, Kelly. *Teaching Adolescent Writers*. Portland, ME: Stenhouse, 2006. Print.

Gawande, Atul. *Complications: A Surgeon's Notes on an Imperfect Science*. New York: Picador, 2003. Print.

Gewertz, Catherine. "Expert Issues Warning on Formative-Assessment Uses." *Education Week* 10 Nov. 2010. Web. 3 May 2011.

———. "Gates, Pearson Partner to Craft Common Core Curriculum." *Education Week* 27 Apr. 2011. Web. 15 June 2011.

Goswami, Dixie, Ceci Lewis, Marty Rutherford, and Diane Waff. *On Teacher Inquiry: Approaches to Language and Literacy Research.* New York: Teachers College, 2009. Print.

Goswami, Dixie, and Peter R. Stillman, eds. *Reclaiming the Classroom: Teacher Research as an Agency for Change.* Portsmouth, NH: Boynton/Cook, 1986. Print.

Graves, Donald H., and Bonnie S. Sunstein, eds. *Portfolio Portraits.* Portsmouth, NH: Heinemann, 1992. Print.

Guskey, Thomas R. "How Classroom Assessments Improve Learning." *Educational Leadership* 60.5 (2003): 6–11. Print.

Hargreaves, Andy, Lorna Earl, Shawn Moore, and Susan Manning. *Learning to Change: Teaching Beyond Subjects and Standards.* San Francisco: Jossey-Bass, 2001. Print.

Harvey, David. *The Condition of Postmodernity: An Enquiry into the Origins of Cultural Change.* New York: Wiley-Blackwell, 1991. Print.

Heifetz, Ronald A. *Leadership without Easy Answers.* Cambridge, MA: Belknap-Harvard UP, 1998. Print.

Herrington, Anne, Kevin Hodgson, and Charles Moran, eds. *Teaching the New Writing: Technology, Change, and Assessment in the 21st-Century Classroom.* New York: Teachers College; Berkeley, CA: National Writing Project, 2009. Print.

Hord, Shirley M. *Professional Learning Communities: What Are They and Why Are They Important? Issues about Change, Volume 6, Number 1.* SEDL, n.d. Web. 13 June 2011. <http://www.sedl.org/pubs/catalog/items/cha35.html>.

Horton, Myles. *The Long Haul: An Autobiography.* New York: Teachers College, 1999. Print.

Hughes, Gerunda B. "Formative Assessment Practices that Maximize Learning for Students at Risk." Andrade and Cizek 212–32.

Huot, Brian. *(Re)Articulating Writing Assessment for Teaching and Learning.* Logan: Utah State UP, 2002. Print.

Huxley, Aldous. *Brave New World.* 1932. New York: Harper Perennial, 1998. Print.

Institute for Educational Leadership. *Leadership for Student Learning: Redefining the Teacher as Leader.* Washington, DC: IEL, 2001. *Institute for Educational Leadership.* Web. 14 June 2001.

International Reading Association/National Council of Teachers of English Joint Task Force on Assessment. *Standards for the Assessment of Reading and Writing.* Rev. ed. Newark, DE: IRA; Urbana, IL: NCTE, 2010. Print.

Keren, Michael. *Blogosphere: The New Political Arena.* Lanham, MD: Lexington Books, 2006. Print.

Koch, Richard, Laura Roop, and Gail Setter. *Statewide and District Professional Development in Standards.* Berkeley, CA: National Writing Project, 2006. *National Writing Project.* Web. 14 June 2011.

Krashen, Stephen. "Comments on the Learn Act." *sdkrashen .com.* Stephen D. Krashen, 2010. Web. 3 May 2011.

Lenhart, Amanda, Sousan Arafeh, Aaron Smith, and Alexandra Rankin Macgill. *Writing, Technology and Teens.* Washington, DC: Pew Internet and American Life Project, 24 Apr. 2008. *College Board.* Web. 3 May 2011.

Lieberman, Ann, and Linda Friedrich. "Teachers, Writers, Leaders." *Educational Leadership* 65.1 (2007): 42–47. Print.

Lieberman, Ann, and Lynne Miller. *Teacher Leadership.* San Francisco: Jossey-Bass, 2004. Print.

Liston, Dan, Jennifer Whitcomb, and Hilda Borko. "NCLB and Scientifically-based Research: Opportunities Lost and Found." *Journal of Teacher Education* 58.2 (2007): 99–107. Print.

Lucido, Horace (Rog). *Educational Genocide: A Plague on Our Children.* Lanham, MD: Rowman and Littlefield, 2010. Print.

Lucido, Joseph. Personal interview. 1 July 2011.

Marshall, Kathie. "What Data-Driven Instruction Should Really Look Like." *Teacher Magazine* 3 June 2009. *National Writing Project.* Web. 14 June 2011.

Marshall, Margaret. *Response to Reform: Composition and the Professionalization of Teaching.* Carbondale: Southern Illinois UP, 2004. Print.

McMillan, James H. "Understanding and Improving Teachers' Classroom Assessment Decision-Making: Implications for Theory and Practice." *Educational Measurement: Issues and Practice* 22.4 (2003): 34–43. Print.

McNeil, Linda M. *Contradictions of School Reform: Educational Costs of Standardized Testing.* New York: Routledge, 2000. Print.

Meyer, Richard J., Linda Brown, Elizabeth DeNino, Kimberly Larson, Mona McKenzie, Kimberly Ridder, and Kimberly Zetterman. *Composing a Teacher Study Group: Learning about Inquiry in Primary Classrooms.* Mahwah, NJ: Erlbaum, 1998. Print.

Mohr, Marian M., Courtney Rogers, Betsy Sanford, Mary Ann Nocerino, Marion S. MacLean, and Sheila Clawson. *Teacher Research for Better Schools.* New York: Teachers College; Berkeley, CA: National Writing Project, 2004. Print.

Nagel, David. "NGLC Pumps Funding into Ed Tech Focused on Common Core." *THE Journal* 14 June 2011. Web. 16 June 2011.

National Council of Teachers of English. *21st Century Literacies: A Policy Research Brief.* NCTE, 2007. Web. 3 May 2011.

———. "The NCTE Definition of 21st Century Literacies." NCTE, 15 Feb. 2008. Web. 3 May 2011.

———. *Reading and Writing Across the Curriculum: A Policy Research Brief.* NCTE, Mar. 2011. Web. 3 May 2011.

National Governors Association and Council of Chief State School Officers. "Designing Common State Assessment Systems." NGA and CCSSO, Apr. 2010. Web. 3 May 2011.

Partnership for 21st Century Skills. *P21.org.* Web. 3 May 2011.

Popham, W. James. "Assessment Literacy Project." Kansas State Department of Education, n.d. Web. 3 May 2011.

———. "Defining and Enhancing Formative Assessment." Consortium for Policy Research in Education, 15 Sept. 2006. Web. 3 May 2011.

Reynolds, Cecilia, ed. *Women in School Leadership: International Perspectives.* Albany: State U of New York P, 2002. Print.

Robb, Laura. *Redefining Staff Development: A Collaborative Model for Teachers and Administrators.* Portsmouth, NH: Heinemann, 2000. Print.

Schön, Donald A. *Educating the Reflective Practitioner: Toward a New Design for Teaching and Learning in the Professions.* San Francisco: Jossey-Bass, 1987. Print.

Sergiovanni, Thomas J. *Building Communities in Schools.* San Francisco: Jossey-Bass, 1994. Print.

SERVE Center. *Classroom Assessment: Assessment Literacy.* U of North Carolina at Greensboro, 2004. Web. 13 June 2011.

Shanton, Kyle D., Marilyn McKinney, Tom Meyer, and Linda
    Friedrich. "Composing Literacy Leadership in Professional
    Development: New Meanings of Practice and Process."
    National Writing Project, 13 May 2010. Web. 14 June
    2011.

Shirky, Clay. *Here Comes Everybody: The Power of Organizing
    without Organizations*. New York: Penguin, 2008. Print.

Spangler, Susan J. Bloome, Michael G. Boyd, Bob Broad, Brian
    Conant, Monica Freaner, Lori Kixmiller, Ann Nussbaum,
    Sarah Paelier, and Christina Wike. "Making Statewide
    Writing Assessment Rigorous, Valid, and Fair: The Illinois
    State Portfolio Assessment of Writing." *Illinois English
    Bulletin* 91.3 (2004): 11–28.

Stiggins, Richard J. "Assessment Literacy for the 21st Century."
    Phi Delta Kappan 77.3 (1995): 238–45. Print.

Strachan, Jane. "Feminist Educational Leadership: Locating
    the Concepts in Practice." *Gender and Education* 11.3 (1999):
    309–22. Print.

Taubman, Peter M. *Teaching by Numbers: Deconstructing the
    Discourse of Standards and Accountability in Education*. New
    York: Routledge, 2009. Print.

Turley, Eric D., and Chris W. Gallagher. "On the *Uses* of
    Rubrics: Reframing the Great Rubric Debate." *English
    Journal* 97.4 (2008): 87–92. Print.

Tyack, David B. *One Best System: A History of American Urban
    Education*. Cambridge, MA: Harvard UP, 1974. Print.

Warnick, Barbara. *Rhetoric Online: Persuasion and Politics on the
    World Wide Web*. New York: Lang, 2007. Print.

Wasley, Patricia A. *Teachers Who Lead: The Rhetoric of Reform
    and the Realities of Practice*. New York: Teachers College,
    2001. Print.

Weinbaum, Alexandra, David Allen, Tina Blythe, Katherine
    Simon, Steve Seidel, and Catherine Rubin. *Teaching as
    Inquiry: Asking Hard Questions to Improve Practice and Student
    Achievement*. New York: Teachers College, 2004. Print.

Weiss, Joann. "The Innovation Mismatch: 'Smart Capital' and
    Education Innovation." Harvard Business Review Blog, 31
    Mar. 2011. Web. 15 June 2011.

Welch, Nancy. *Living Room: Teaching Writing in a Privatized
    World*. Portsmouth, NH: Boynton/Cook, 2008. Print.

Westheimer, Joel. *Among Schoolteachers: Community, Autonomy,
    and Ideology in Teachers' Work*. New York: Teachers College,
    2008. Print.

White, Edward M. "The Scoring of Writing Portfolios: Phase
    2." *College Composition and Communication* 56.4 (2005):
    581–600. Print.

Wiliam, Dylan. "An Integrative Summary of the Research
    Literature and Implications for a New Theory of Formative
    Assessment." Andrade and Cizek 18–40.

Wilson, Maja. *Rethinking Rubrics in Writing Assessment*. Ports-
    mouth, NH: Heinemann, 2006. Print.

Yancey, Kathleen Blake. "Looking Back as We Look Forward:
    Historicizing Writing Assessment as a Rhetorical Act."
    College Composition and Communication 50.3 (1999): 483–503.
    Print.

———. "Made Not Only in Words: Composition in a New
    Key." *College Composition and Communication* 56.2 (2004):
    297–328. Print.

Index

Authors

Chris W. Gallagher is Writing Program director and professor of English at Northeastern University, where he teaches graduate and undergraduate courses in writing and rhetoric. He is the author of three previous books: *Radical Departures: Composition and Progressive Pedagogy* (2002); *Reclaiming Assessment: A Better Alternative to the Accountability Agenda* (2007); and, with Amy Lee, *Teaching Writing That Matters: Tools and Projects That Motivate Adolescent Writers* (2008). He also has published numerous articles on teaching and assessing writing in journals such as *College Composition and Communication, College English*, and *JAC*, as well as articles on educational assessment in journals such as *Phi Delta Kappan* and *Educational Leadership*. Gallagher lives near Boston with his family.

Eric D. Turley teaches English classes at Kirkwood High School in Kirkwood, Missouri. He has taught writing and literature courses at both secondary and postsecondary levels and has published articles in *English Journal* and *Phi Delta Kappan*. His dissertation, *The Scientific Management of Writing and the Residue of Reform*, was awarded the CCCC James Berlin Memorial Outstanding Dissertation Award. He lives in Webster Groves, Missouri, with his wife and their children.

This book was typeset in Janson Text and BotonBQ by
Barbara Frazier.

Typefaces used on the cover include American Typewriter,
Frutiger Bold, Formata Light, and Formata Bold.

The book was printed on 60-lb. Recycled Offset paper
by Versa Press, Inc.